French Garden Style

French Garden Style

Georges Lévêque
Marie-Françoise Valéry

BARRON'S

New York Toronto

French Garden Style
First U.S. edition published by Barron's Educational
Series, Inc
© Frances Lincoln Limited 1990
Original French text © Marie-Françoise Valéry 1990
English translation copyright © Frances Lincoln Limited 1990
Photographs © Georges Lévêque 1990

French Garden Style was conceived, edited and produced by
Frances Lincoln Limited
Apollo Works, 5 Charlton Kings Road, London NW5 2SB

International Standard Book Number: 0-8120-6157-8
Library of Congress Catalog Card No. 90-35434

Library of Congress Cataloging-in-Publication Data
Lévêque, Georges.
French garden style/Georges Lévêque, Marie-Françoise
Valéry:
(translated from the French by Anne Atkinson).
   p.   cm.
  "First U.S. edition"—T.p. verso.
  ISBN 0-8120-6157-8
  1. Gardens. French   I. Valéry, Marie-
Françoise.   II. Title.
SB457.65.L48 1991
712'.0944—dc20

All inquiries should be addressed to:
Barron's Educational Series, Inc.
250 Wireless Boulevard, Hauppauge, New York 11788

PRINTED IN SINGAPORE
0123 9870 987654321

PAGE 1

*A vista, through the arched gateways which diminish in
size to increase the length of the perspective, leads through a
succession of walled gardens at Canon, in northern France.
The park was designed in the mid-eighteenth century by
the owner at that time, Elie de Beaumont, who drew
inspiration from Kew Gardens and the park at Stowe in
England. Grapes, peaches, apples, pears, almonds and figs
ripened within these sheltered enclosures, named Les
Chartreuses after the Carthusian Covent in Paris which
supplied most of the fruit trees. Today the gardens are filled
with flowers – colourful drifts of red and pink dahlias,
pansies, phlox, cosmos, coreopsis, heleniums and solidagos
thrive in an area once devoted to the table.*

PAGE 2

*Made in the 1950s around the seventeenth-century
château, the gardens of La Mormaire are a combination of
formal French structure and permissive English planting
with touches of Italian elegance. The strict architectural
symmetry of the clipped hedges in yew, hornbeam and box
is relieved by the curves and 'windows' and by the
deliberately off-centre placing of the glaucous cedar tree;
and the highly disciplined layout is softened by the muted
colours of the massed, informal planting within the
flowerbeds.*

OPPOSITE

*A field of vibrant wild flowers flourishing at Dampierre.
Although the original gardens and park surrounding the
seventeenth-century château were designed by Le Nôtre, a
completely new natural garden was created in the wildest
part of the park in the 1980s. This provides an unfailing
succession of flowers from spring until autumn – expansive
drifts of colour in meadows and woodland, and beside lawns
and streams. Snowdrops, crocuses, narcissi, scillas, bluebells
and tulips are followed by irises and a profusion of eremurus.
Azaleas and rhododendrons, colonies of wild flowers such as
primroses, foxgloves, columbines, monkey musk, loosestrife
and agrimony are happy in the shade of tall trees, while the
meadows are invaded by wild grasses, ox-eye daisies, meadowsweet, poppies and cornflowers.*

*I dedicate this book to Le Vicomte de Noailles, today no longer with us,
to his family and his numerous friends, for the unfailing support, help and encouragement
and for the invaluable advice which they have constantly and generously afforded me.* G.L.

Clematis armandii *growing in the garden of the Villa Noailles.*

Contents

Foreword

For years we have seen French gardening through eyes blinkered by historical precedent. Horace Walpole writing in the 1770s, a hundred years after Versailles was laid out, admits that 'When a Frenchman reads of the Garden of Eden, I do not doubt but he concludes it was something approaching to that of Versailles, with clipped hedges, berceaus, and trellis work.' Those of us with a different vision of Eden believe that Versailles epitomizes French style. We may even believe that all French gardens since the 1660s, both great and small, have been laid out using similar rules of formality and perspective. Indeed, the term 'French Gardening' has been synonymous with Versailles itself and with the countless eighteenth-century 'French' gardens scattered throughout the courts of Europe and as far as the shores of the Baltic at Leningrad.

Versailles has sweeping vistas stretching to the horizon above steps, statuary and water basins and canals which reflect the sky and buildings to contrast with the sound and movement of sparkling cascades and fountains; tightly clipped allées and fine sculptures frame the distant vistas. As Alexander Pope observed, all was based on symmetry – 'Each alley has a brother, and half the garden just reflects the other.' At the time the whole vast project was also intended to glorify Louis XIV himself. The Sun King's vast self-importance and need to demonstrate his power encapsulates our image of the French garden. It is the most famous garden in the world, the epitome of the seventeenth-century Baroque in which the geometric Italian Renaissance garden, with terraces on steep hillsides and intimate enclosed garden rooms aligned round a villa, was extended to encompass the whole countryside and to emphasize man's total control over nature and, in particular, Louis's wealth and power. Whether Versailles marks the high moment of a serious art form or was a great folly, we cannot deny either its monumental, if cold, beauty, nor its influence. It probably was and still is the most important formal garden in the world but even contemporaries could ridicule its splendours and the Sun King's *folies-de-grandeur* where, with water scarce to mock the grandeur, fountains could only operate in turn for the king's royal progress. Within a hundred years Horace Walpole described it as 'littered with statues and fountains . . . the gardens of a great child'.

Our ideas of French design even extend to the realms of purer horticulture; man, not only content to prove his power over nature with avenues clipped to stretch through ancient forests, sought to further manipulate it by controlling and shaping living plants in the garden itself. Le Nôtre's gardeners pleached and sheered hornbeams, chestnuts and lime trees to make smooth walls of green – the famous *charmilles* which still decorate many of the vast layouts – and topiary box, yew and bay matched the glistening marble or more solemn stone statuary. At Versailles even tender myrtle was clipped for annual insertion in the box parterres and, of course, citrus fruit, arrayed like troops on parade in ornamental tubs, were trimmed into round or pyramidal heads for summer display on the terrace of the *Orangerie*. The French mastered the art of pruning fruit trees both for beauty and for productivity; in this ancient art they have always been teachers. For centuries French pattern books have given instructions for espaliers, cordons, palmettes and complicated diamond shaped profiles.

Of course this book, in which many gardens developed by owners with a very different idea of the Garden of Eden are described and illustrated, will be an eye-opener to those steeped in Versailles-style Frenchness. These paradise gardens are more akin to the Dutch Jan Brueghel's vision of Eden portrayed in a painting (almost contemporary with Versailles), in which flowers and fruits are borne in tropical profusion and man and animals, at peace with each other, roam freely among the glades of a parklike landscape. Many of them are personal and private expressions of a search for this ideal.

And yet there is a thread of formality which appears and reappears like the repetition of a phrase in music or in poetry. Today the best French gardening seems to combine features from several gardening traditions. In general, although often disguised by informal planting styles, each garden has a firm overall structure; meticulous attention to detail and an emphasis on topiary plant shapes and fruit tree manipulation seem uniquely French in spirit. Even in the descriptions of the most romantic and voluptuous gardens where English cottage plants jostle each other in Jekyllian ecstasy, there is a distinctive Frenchness of control.

Without being a history book *French Garden Style* reveals aspects of French gardening development through the centuries; in the most modern gardens it is still clear that history plays a role in shaping garden structure. In it there is a fine balance of gardens chosen from both the 'old' and the 'new'. The 'old' have modern planting while the 'new' incorporate historical features. The book is a celebration of French gardening today, yet through the descriptive writing we capture echoes of evolving styles which, without leaving Versailles-like formality entirely to one side, encompass the *jardins anglais-chinois* of the late eighteenth century, the Hausmann parks and boulevards of nineteenth-century Paris, with their elaborate beds of tender flowers and foliage plants, and more Robinsonian 'natural' planting schemes adapted to the different climatic regions. In the present day some French gardeners, disciplined by historical precedent, create new masterpieces in which hardy plants contained in quite structured layouts tumble and flow to rival the triumphs of Edwardian England. Other twentieth-century gardens reflect individual taste and sometimes eccentricity; above all they express a preference for exquisite detailing both in design and flowers. The French have learnt the joys of emulating nature but, keeping firm overall control, are less subservient to 'naturalism' than modern gardeners in England or in North America who dabble with purposeless meandering curves and native plant material.

In his *The Education of a Gardener* Russell Page wrote that 'Garden-making, like gardening itself, concerns the relationship of the human being to his natural surroundings. The idiom has changed from place to place and from one period to another, whether we consider the smallest medieval herb garden ..22 or the enormous perspectives which Le Nôtre cut through the gentle slopes and forests of the Ile de France.' In this book we see French garden styles revealed to underline Russell Page's truth. Monet's long narrow flower-filled beds at Giverny are full of colour but, in essence, are laid out on the same grid system as a medieval monastic herb garden. Villandry's vegetable patchwork quilt and terraced allegorical gardens, a 'reconstruction' of this century, are based on du Cerceau's interpretations of the Renaissance garden, a hundred years before Le Nôtre worked at Versailles. In the south at La Chèvre d'Or old olive terraces echo Italian formality and provide the strong lines and perspective which frame the exotic tender plants from all corners of the world that thrive in the mild climate. At Eyrignac clipped geometric shapes 'calculated to the last inch' define space with living 'green' architecture in eighteenth-century style; it is a fine restoration, a garden rescued from nineteenth-century neglect.

Other gardens reflect a passion for plants and their collection; these convey the more naturalistic aspects of French gardening. There is a wilderness of beauty on the Cherbourg peninsula where tropical-type exotics flourish in romantic profusion. At Kerdalo in Brittany a plantsman's garden is contained in a framework of old walls and terraces. Even where the most informal gardens have been made by foreigners there is an element of French control in the garden's firm organization. The garden in the Ile de France was made by an American brought up in a wild woodland garden in New England; the planting freedom is tamed by French-style box hedges and paths which define space. Le Vastiveral is a Robinsonian garden near Dieppe created by the Romanian Princess Sturdza; colourful island beds are meticulous in every detail. La Serre de la Madone on the Riviera evolved as a collector's paradise for the American owner of Hidcote Manor in England but its layout reflects the scheme of the existing terraces which drop below the villa. At La Garoupe, first laid out by the Aberconways at the turn of the century, rare and tender plants as well as encroaching native *maquis* soften quite formal pattern-making.

Marie-Françoise Valéry's evocative descriptions of significant gardens, set in the royal forests of the north, in Normandy orchards, in the more rolling hills of Burgundy or in the hot and dry aromatic *maquis* of the south are perfectly captured by George Lévêque's camera. The pictures reflect the ambiance of each garden's setting and emphasize the differences between cold northern light and clear pink-toned sun-hazed Mediterranean tints. At Royaumont the sky is grey and misty, at La Garoupe the heat is intense and burning, only relieved by glimpses of the adjacent blue Mediterranean. With the camera we wander into gardens such as the formal 'green' Eyrignac, decorated with Versailles-like hornbeam *charmilles* and vistas, and delight in its humanized modern scale; gentle flower colours revealed at Les Trois Pommes reflect a more English garden mood. In this book writing and pictures convey the vast range of gardening possibilities in the different regions of France; they do far more than that in leading us through gardens scenes where owners have seized and tamed nature to create very special effects of beauty and imagination. Although we will never forget the splendour of Versailles, we now know that French gardening has more to offer than a repetition or regurgitation of the formal ethic. We go to France with a newly awakened anticipation of delight.

Penelope Hobhouse
Tintinhull, 1990

Classic Formality

Formal garden design, with its emphasis on a disciplined and architectural layout, can trace its roots to the classical gardens of antiquity. Whether seen at its most majestic at a great château like Courances or at its most charming in a simple, colourful parterre, formality is governed by universal characteristics. Nature is tamed, controlled and ordered and given little scope for waywardness or initiative. Even the ground is leveled, every undulation smoothed out and each gradient planned into imposing terraces linked, usually, by elaborate flights of steps. Water is used either for its reflective qualities or for impressive displays of cascades and fountains. Lawns are contained in rectangular frames; trees stand in straight lines; and shrubs are rigorously pruned into ornamental shapes like the pyramids and cones at Eyrignac. The visitor is invited to walk along straight avenues and to gaze down vistas which either lead to an eye-catching focal point, or seem to reach the sky at the horizon. Statues, stone ornaments and treillage are sometimes the only flourishes allowed, but these, too, contribute to the sense of permanence and stability.

These are gardens which appeal to the mind as well as the eye. The mastery of geometry, symmetry and perspective produces compositions of superb balance. It is not suprising that, although the style reached its apogee in France with the work of Le Nôtre, its principles have had such a deep and lasting appeal.

The rigorously controlled pattern – with its matching pairs of motifs – of one of the ornamental parterres at Villandry focuses on a fountain set in a wall niche. The ephemeral quality of the forget-me-nots, wallflowers and tulips emphasizes the permanence and discipline of the immaculately-pruned box and yew.

Courances

Courances: appropriately, even the place-name suggests the sight and sound of running water for it is the ripple and murmur of water, the sound of waterfalls and the reflections in the ornamental pools that bring this otherwise very stately formal garden vibrantly to life.

Set in a region that has always benefited from the nearby presence of the royal château of Fontainebleau – with its military and equestrian traditions and incomparably rich artistic heritage – the early seventeenth-century château of Courances is pure Louis XIII in style. It uses three of the period's favourite materials – Fontainebleau sandstone, grey slate and rose-pink brick – in a symmetrical, soberly decorated design, with the tall chimneys and steeply pitched, pointed roofs much loved by seventeenth-century architects. Set on the edge of a forest that Corot painted, no less than eleven springs emerge here, providing water in quantity and of exceptionally high quality. Indeed, its clarity and purity had such a reputation that, when Fontainebleau was a royal residence, water was specially brought from Courances for the King's children to drink.

Other French formal gardens have similar advantages, of course, the most famous being the Grandes Eaux at Versailles. But there, because of insufficient water pressure, Louis XIV had to call on the latest hydraulic technology to feed all the magnificent cascades which were intended to flow day and night. At Courances, the fountains need no machinery to set them going – the creator of the gardens had simply to tap the natural power of the emerging springs. In the eighteenth century, Jacques Dulaure wrote an admiring description: 'Nature has created this effect of ever-flowing water, an effect far superior to those pompous cascades which by mighty effort live for a moment and then die down, as if a painting were to vanish all at once from its frame.' Waterfalls, pools

and canals are linked by underground pipes and finally run into the river Ecole as it flows through meadows where white fences enclose a few quietly grazing horses.

Expanses of water are a recurring feature at Courances, often brilliantly combined with imposing vistas. As you come through the main entrance along the Allée d'Honneur – an avenue edged with lawns – canals on either side reflect the magnificent 'listed' plane trees; on the other side of the château is Le Miroir, a long formal stretch of water which, on fine days, reflects the whole façade. Beyond it is a round basin with a statue of children riding a dolphin set in the middle. Further still, beyond the huge main lawn, a semi-circle of grass which curves behind a round pool, Le Rond de Moigny, closes the main vista. The château itself appears to be surrounded by moats, but in fact is built on a natural island; another shady avenue, the Allée de la Table, leads to a ten-sided pool known as La Gerbe beyond which stretches Le Grand Canal. More water appears as a series of small cascades, called Les Nappes, which tumble into the Grand Canal. To the left of the château, overlooking the so-called horseshoe pool, Le Fer à Cheval, stands a marble statue of the nymph Arethusa, originally made for the royal park at Marly, near Versailles, by the sculptor Poirier. Water spouts of Fontainebleau sandstone feed water into the moat. Shaped like dolphin heads, they are a rare sight and may have been inspired by Italian originals or were carved by Italian craftsmen brought in to work at nearby Fontainebleau. Further left still, near La Foulerie – a charming building facing an Anglo-Japanese garden – you come to the Presbytère pool from where you can glimpse the spire of the village church.

Around the white, grey and rose-pink château, the dominant colours of the park are grey, blue and green: the grey of the sandstone, the blue of water, the green of

foliage. Oak, lime, yew, beech, ash, horse-chestnut and hornbeam are the species that predominate; box, in both large and small varieties, also does well; and, most notable of all, as soon as you enter the garden, are the majestic plane trees. A work of art in themselves, they were planted as long ago as 1782 and now have such a vast span of branches that they seem to defy the laws of equilibrium. Monsieur and Madame de Ganay, the present owners of the château, become nervous about the trees whenever a gale or thunderstorm threatens.

The design of the park is attributed to André Le Nôtre but, since the estate has changed hands so often and the archives are lost, we cannot be certain of his involvement. During the two hundred years since its creation, the park has suffered increasingly from neglect, but at the end of the nineteenth century it was restored by Achille Duchêne, the architect and landscape gardener who revived many properties, including Blenheim in England, Breteuil in Belgium and Vaux-le-Vicomte in France. Duchêne was meticulous in following original plans, but the final effect carries his personal imprint. Thanks to him and to the Marquise de Ganay, the present owner's grandmother who commissioned Duchêne, Courances came back to life.

Setting aside one or two minor variations, Courances is the epitome of the French formal garden style in which château and environment form a whole. The house, which represents the owner's authority, stands in command of its surroundings. To emphasize its subordinate position, the entire park is visible from the château, as at Vaux-le-Vicomte, and natural features appear tamed, the trees and plants rigorously pruned and trained.

Inside, the château seems transparent; light pours in through the many huge windows. From the main reception rooms, you have only to turn your head to see, on one side, the view over the Miroir d'Eau and, on the other, the long prospect down the avenue to the main entrance. From these rooms, too, you can look down on to the magnificent *parterres de broderie* with their delicate curlicues of box.

Two of the guiding principles of formal gardening – balance and symmetry – are evident wherever you look: the twin canals which border the Allée d'Honneur, the mirror-image pair of *parterres de broderie*, the two avenues running off at angles from the château and the symmetrical rows of statues beside the Miroir d'Eau are obvious examples. They are also features much favoured by Le Nôtre: the Grand Canal, in particular, was an essential ingredient of his designs, as at Vaux-le-Vicomte, Chantilly and Sceaux. He was masterly in his use of shimmering expanses of water – canals, pools and lakes – both to reflect their surroundings and, most importantly, the sky, and to provide a background of ripples and murmurs. Such was his aesthetic and technical control of flowing water that he gave all his gardens a magical, vibrant atmosphere.

From the main reception rooms of the château the overall view is stupendous; but there are also surprises in store as you walk round the park. A series of little waterfalls suddenly becomes visible as you turn a corner or you find yourself quite unexpectedly facing yet another geometrically shaped pool. Even the symmetry leaves room for subtle variations: one avenue, the Allée de la Table, leads to a round pond, while its twin ends with a circle of grass. In formal French gardens paths are normally covered in gravel, but here at Courances many are turfed. Nature has also been allowed some latitude, even though the architectural outlines are preserved. If Le Nôtre could now see the billowing tops of the lime trees round the Miroir, he would perhaps prune them back into neater shapes, but in fact the present irregular natural growth helps to soften the rigidly rectilinear effect.

In complete contrast to the rest of the park, and to the concept of French formality, is the Anglo-Japanese garden. It was designed by Berthe de Béhague, Marquise de Ganay, grandmother of the present

RIGHT
Built in the early seventeenth century, the château is situated on a natural island. This and the surrounding land has been so shaped that the water appears as a formal moat.

Marquis, with the advice of an English gardening friend. In spring, there is an array of subtle colour from all the naturalized bulbs, and later from Judas tree blossom, *Hyacinthoides hispanica* (syn. *Scilla campanulata*), Foxgloves, herbaceous geraniums and peonies; then, in autumn, acer leaves take over with a flamboyant spectrum of colour from brilliant gold to carmine red, with every possible tawny shade between.

Monsieur and Madame de Ganay and their children are all much attached to Courances and their affection for the place shows in the impeccable way it is maintained and is conveyed by its sympathetic atmosphere. Madame de Ganay, who is president of the Société des Amateurs des Jardins and very knowledgeable on the subject of gardens and flowers, has continued to develop the garden. Near the château she has planted groups of grey and silver plants and pale-coloured roses such as 'New Dawn', 'Mermaid' and 'Canary Bird'. On suitable walls she has trained magnolias and hydrangeas such as the *H. petiolaris*, which is now climbing up the sides of a charming Louis XIII pavilion beside the entrance. Well chosen plants like these help to enhance the beauty of the garden and its evolving life.

The visitor to Courances cannot help being affected by its special ambience, which comes from such experiences as the sight of a dappled sky reflected in a sparkling sheet of water, a glimpse down a regal avenue of trees which seems to stretch to infinity, the sweet smell of 'Aloha' roses, philadelphus and clumps of scented geraniums, but most of all from the seductive sound of the constant, but gentle movement of water.

Thury-Harcourt

No two gardens can ever be the same, though some draw inspiration from other gardens and betray similar influences. Thury-Harcourt, however, is strikingly original. A completely new kind of formal garden, it is the creation of the present Duc d'Harcourt. In his book, *Des Jardins Heureux*, a personal and lucid treatise on the art of gardening, the Duke advocates a sensitive approach to nature and at Thury-Harcourt he has succeeded in making a garden that reflects his views and appeals to both the mind and the senses.

The small formal part of the garden of Thury-Harcourt lies within an historic park surrounded by Normandy pasture-land. As soon as one goes through the gates, the castle ruins offer a reminder of past glories: fire damage, revolution and war have brought down the great stone buildings, but the Duc d'Harcourt has allowed nature rather than the restorer the upper hand here. He has, however, restored and extended another building – originally used as a pleasure pavilion – as a house for himself, and created an astonishing new garden within the estate.

The rolling parkland was redesigned and newly planted during the 1950s. The different walks that have been cut through the park – the Allée des Pervenches (periwinkles), the Allée des Merisiers (wild cherries), and the Allée de Mai (May) – are turfed and bordered with bulbs and flowering shrubs. These entice the visitor to walk around the park and along the banks of the river Orne, then, twisting, suddenly bring you out above a brilliantly coloured garden whose geometric layout comes as a marvellous surprise.

A rectangular clearing defined by trees and hedges encloses a swathe of green turf embroidered with ribbons of flowers in a simple pattern of four rectangles which soften into a circle where their corners meet in the centre. Unlike other formal schemes where pattern is delineated in

It is hard to believe that this colourful profusion of summer flowers can belong to a formal garden, though the pastel shades and brighter accents of this glorious mixture of cosmos, dahlias, leucanthemums, delphiniums and campanulas are clearly chosen for deliberate effect. In fact, it is the placing of what appears to be an informal arrangement within the exact lines of a symmetrically formal ground plan that makes this garden so stylish and unique.

clipped green (often box) and occasionally filled with colourful flowers, here the pattern is formed by bands of colour which enclose areas of smooth emerald grass; thus it is essentially a summer garden and so – again contrary to most formal schemes – is not placed close to the house where it could be seen during the winter. If you wonder why its geometric pattern appears so satisfying, the simple answer is that the Duc d'Harcourt has designed it according to the Golden Section, the formula devised by the Greeks for calculating rectangular shapes. Inexplicably, the use of the ratio of approximately 1 to 1.62 always produces harmonious effects. In creating these balanced patterns the Duke has shown remarkable architectural skill. His artistic and rhythmic sense are equally evident: the first in his handling of colour; the second in the ordering of pink-flowered shrubs in the centre and blue in the outer corners of the borders.

The flowers that fill these narrow beds are a heady mixture of plants, chosen to provide a succession of blooms and colour from the beginning of summer until the first frosts. Any which settle happily are allowed to stay: dahlias, herbaceous plants (phlox, monarda, nepeta) and shrubs (roses and hibiscus) mingle with annuals (*Salvia farinacea*, cosmos, lavatera, zinnias, cleomes) so that each year brings subtle changes. The scheme is controlled by colour – a few touches of yellow, red and orange lighten the whole effect, but it is pastel that predominates. The long borders have three rows of plants, the tallest in the middle. Among the tallest are blue asters which gradually take over from marvellous mauve delphiniums. These slightly sombre tones need the addition of pink, as well as touches of white to point up the many transitions and associations of colour.

All our senses are affected here – our sight of course, our sense of smell with the scent of flowers, hearing with the sound of

Classic Formality: Thury-Harcourt

BELOW
This detail shows how carefully controlled are the colour effects, with the pastel tones of the borders, like the peachy pink of these dahlias, being perfectly set against the rich green of the rectangles of grass in between.

RIGHT
An overview of the garden shows the simple formality of the design, whose originality lies in the planting. Formerly a kitchen garden, the site is sheltered and framed by the surrounding trees. Being on a single level, it is truly a parterre.

birds, even touch in the way the grass yields under our feet. There is also an intellectual satisfaction in trying to work out the ideas underlying the design of this garden. In his book, the Duc d'Harcourt explains how he has tried to convey a sympathy with the natural environment, to remain in tune with the weather, type of soil, periods of sunshine, flowering times, and with those plants which grow well here. In accordance with his view that 'a beautiful garden is made with love, one in which personal preferences always give way to the special demands of a place', he has, with fastidious understanding and self-effacement, acted as a catalyst for 'Nature's secret wishes'. He also describes a beautiful garden as one that provokes 'a sense of wonder, an instant of happiness, a momentary feeling of perfection against a background of transience', and indeed the formal garden at Thury-Harcourt is one of those places which breathes a sense of order and serenity; so enduring is its satisfaction that here one may have 'intimations of immortality'.

Eyrignac

Eyrignac is a masterly example of the living architecture of shrubs and trees; its majestic green lines, perfect proportions and clipped geometric shapes are calculated to the last inch. Its layout, based on three main vistas – one at right angles to two that are parallel to each other – is relatively simple and compact. But components of the garden are so well thought-out and are executed with such éclat that it appears to be far more complex than it is. It is a remarkable illustration of eighteenth-century French formality – its imposing grandeur tempered by decorative details of great charm.

Few people knew of Eyrignac's existence until the present owner, Patrick Sermadiras de Pouzols de Lile, began to open it to the public in the 1980s. For many people it comes as a great surprise to discover this exquisite garden in the heart of the Péri-gord, where the climate and terrain are difficult and where decorative gardens are rare. Created in the eighteenth century by a member of his family, it went through a strange exotic phase of bamboos and palm trees in the nineteenth century, then became run down and neglected. In the 1950s Patrick Sermadiras' father decided to restore it, following the original eighteenth-century plans by an Italian decorative artist called Ricci; the work has been carried out gradually since then. Eventually the property was handed over to Patrick Sermadiras, who has become completely devoted to this extraordinary place.

The garden is all green – a glorious blend of every possible green with light and shadow playing over the clipped patterns to produce yet more variations of colour. Tonal intensity varies with leaf texture, from the clear fresh green of grass kept watered by a sprinkler system, through the glossy leaves of box, and the slightly transluscent foliage of hornbeam, to the matt, almost black needles of yew.

As you walk out of the manor house,

OPPOSITE

The immaculate, geometric lines of the garden are clear from this view – from the manor house – over the eighteenth-century box scroll-work on the lawn. The vista along the avenue of yew obelisks has been deftly manipulated so that optically it appears longer.

RIGHT

The hornbeam walk, the Allée des Charmes, is a superb exercise in contrasting sculptural forms. On each side of the walk, precisely matching cylindrical yews are almost encircled by the curving buttresses of hornbeam.

built in the Périgord style, you come into a formal courtyard with sand raked smooth twice a day and a pool edged with box set against a retaining wall. Two flights of stone steps lead up to the main garden, where box hedging makes an elegant scrolled pattern on well-mown turf. Beyond this is an avenue of two-hundred-year-old yews clipped into pointed cones. It seems strangely protracted – curved steps running up the slopes gradually become smaller, deluding the eye with the apparently lengthened perspective.

As one turns left, through the box scrolls, the garden opens into the Allée des Charmes, a magnificent walk where dense buttresses of hornbeam are regularly interspersed with cylindrical columns of yew in a design of rigorous grandeur. The view culminates in a Chinese pavilion – as was traditional in eighteenth-century designs. Walking along the allée, a detour to the left gives you a glimpse of a pool and of a pavilion in the same regional style as the manor, both secluded in a green 'room' formed by hornbeam hedges. Further

In the Allée des Vases, which runs parallel with the hornbeam walk, rows of pyramidal cypresses back a monumental serpentine yew hedge. Within each scallop is a topiary yew growing in a large terracotta pot – the 'vases' which lend their name to the avenue. The contrast of shapes and textures is accentuated by the play of light, and so despite the lack of any other colour but green, the effect is astonishingly rich. The manor house is just visible at the end of the walk beyond wrought iron gates.

along the allée there is another opening into an orchard in which Patrick Sermadiras has a collection of red-fruited apple trees clipped into mopheads, their feet fringed by grey santolina.

Turning left, before reaching the Chinese pavilion, you walk down a cross-axis path leading to a recently planted enclosure. Here the surrounding hornbeam hedge is pierced by 'windows' through which are views over the fields and hillsides round Sarlat. From here another glorious avenue, the Allée des Vases, which runs parallel to the Allée des Charmes, entices you on. A line of tall cypresses stands behind a substantial serpentine yew hedge. Within each of its indentations is a terracotta vase planted with a topiary yew in the shape of a cake stand topped by a finial ball. A pair of matching fountains facing each other across the path gives an Italianate effect.

The Allée des Vases takes you to another green 'room' – a circle of trees surrounding a scroll pattern of box – and from here you make your way back to the house through a little open-air boudoir, a cool place to sit under tall trees with an orchestra of cicadas playing in the background.

Patrick Sermadiras can never have anticipated the importance of this garden in his life. Eyrignac is now his creation. He was born there and grew up among the elaborate topiary cones and columns. He walks round the garden several times a day, even sometimes at night if he chances to arrive back late after an unduly long absence. From Paris, where he works as an editor of art books, he will often telephone the gardeners twice a day. Thus he knows every line, every angle and curve, in the minutest detail. According to Madame de Maintenon, Louis XIV hated even the smallest twig to look out of place; the same

might be said of Patrick Sermadiras, although his feelings are based on a close understanding of nature rather than an antipathy to its whims.

Yews and box are clipped twice a year, hornbeams four times. Occasionally trees need rejuvenating, sometimes by what amounts to a surgical operation. The yews in the Allée des Charmes date back to the eighteenth century and have had to be cut back hard to encourage dense foliage. The gardeners who carry out the work are enormously skilful, using only cords, templates and manual shears. No electrical equipment is used.

It is this kind of close attention that contributes to the spell-binding atmosphere at Eyrignac. It is clear to any visitor that this garden is not just a virtuoso exercise in pattern and formality but a place that is lived in and cared for with fervent passion.

Villandry

Balzac described the province of Touraine as a work of art in its own right. Some mysterious alchemy seems to have placed a spell on the gentle landscape: the pale Loire sand, the white stonework and gleaming slate roofs, and the hundreds of châteaux in their green, leafy settings – all seem to be bathed in a special quality of light. Villandry, with its justly celebrated geometrically laid out gardens, lies in the very centre of the province and is one of its greatest treasures.

The sixteenth-century château, built by and for Jean Le Breton, a finance minister of François I, has three main buildings, forming a horseshoe round the central courtyard. Successive owners, in particular the Marquis de Castellane, and a brother of Napoleon, brought about many unfortunate changes. Some built additions in the worst possible taste, others surrounded the château with a vaguely 'English' landscape garden quite out of keeping with Villandry's essentially French, very exact and formal aesthetic traditions.

Both the château and its immense gardens recovered their former pure lines thanks to Doctor Joachim Carvallo, a scholarly man, Spanish in origin, who had married a wealthy American. They bought the château in 1906 and, together, used their money and talents to revive and restore this remarkable work of art, replanning the gardens according to the original designs made in the sixteenth century by Androuet du Cerceau.

Villandry is a garden for the intellect, a place possessing all the Cartesian rigour and clarity, the sense of measure and proportion that characterize a certain French cast of mind. A few embellishments, such as fountains and some statuary here and there, suggest Renaissance Italy, but most of all, Villandry brings to mind the formality of the enclosed monastic gardens of the Middle Ages, the *jardins de curé*, with their trelliswork, neat beds of

OPPOSITE
The intricate, yet tightly controlled patterns of the famous Potager are best seen from a raised viewpoint. Trellised arbours for climbing roses and quadrilobed pools with single jets of water mark the intersections of the paths which are covered in local gravel. Outlined in low clipped box, the beds are filled with subtle colour from the leaves of different vegetables. Brighter colours come from the flowers in narrow beds which surround each major square of the design. In the background is a shaded walk for viewing the garden, and a glimpse of houses in the village beyond.

ABOVE
A detail of one of the beds shows a pleasing contrast between red salad foliage and the dense green box hedging. Closely pruned fruit trees punctuate the ends of the paths, and add height to the design.

BELOW
These enormous cabbages, which form part of the mosaic pattern, change colour in autumn and continue looking decorative until Christmas.

ABOVE
The complex series of decorative, evergreen parterres is on the same level as the reception rooms of the château, and was devised to look interesting all through the year, and indeed a sense of immutability and timelessness is conveyed by the perfect balance and strict formality of the design. The parterres in the foreground symbolize the four aspects of Love and, beyond them, below the raised walk, are the patterns of the 'Cross' garden. On the higher level, beyond the pleached lime avenue, is the water garden.

vegetables, medicinal herbs and flowers for altar decoration. From the terraces overlooking the estate, you can look down on the five hectares (twelve and a half acres) of gardens as if they were a picture in a frame, and pick out the varied influences and the ways they are blended.

Protected on three sides by the château, the church and the village, and by outbuildings to the north, the gardens look south up towards a flat expanse of water, the *pièce d'eau*, and to countryside beyond. A spring is the source of water for the *pièce d'eau*, which then feeds the canal and fountains further down. The ornamental gardens, divided by the canal, are on a level with the main reception rooms of the château, and a potager is lower down, on a level with the outbuildings and stables. Each of the three gardens – the water, the ornamental parterres and the Potager – is surrounded and overlooked by a shaded path, where visitors walk under arching lime trees and pergolas hung with vines.

The ornamental gardens are designed as a series of complex parterres: closest to the house is the Jardin d'Amour, an allegory of the four kinds of love, laid out beneath tall clipped yews, delineated in immaculately clipped box. Tragic Love is symbolized by sword and dagger shapes, Adulterous Love with fans, Tender Love has hearts separated by flames, while Passionate Love is represented by broken hearts. Beyond this are box parterres in the form of ingeniously traced crosses – of Malta, Languedoc and the Basque country. Bedding plants such as pansies, forget-me-nots, tulips, dahlias and rudbeckias ensure that there is always bright colour filling the spaces within the green outlines.

On the west side of the canal is the Deuxième Salon, another series of box parterres in the form of motifs connected with music or representing stylized instruments. Here the colours that fill the pattern are softer: spears of iris bring a luminous, silky blue in spring, while lavender and grey santolina make an elegant, more permanent contribution.

At a slightly lower level, to the west of the château, is the Potager. Covering half a hectare (about an acre of land), it is divided into nine enormous squares, each surrounded by trellised fencing – much of which is covered in espaliered fruit trees – and containing a well-defined, intricate design outlined in box: the crosses, Greek keys, rectangles and L-shapes seem almost like mazes. Height is given to the design by standard roses, by clipped fruit trees and by trellised arbours of climbing roses at the corners where the paths intersect. The paths are covered in the local Loire gravel, known as 'Mignonnette', and small quadri-lobed pools with simple jets of water stand at the crossings.

Today the vegetables are carefully chosen by Madame Carvallo, whose husband Robert, the present owner, is the grandson of Joachim Carvallo. Madame brings about some spectacular effects by orchestrating the colours of the vegetables and their foliage – greens, yellows, oranges, reds, purples and blue-greys. The effects are further enriched by the inclusion of some brightly coloured annuals and by carefully thought-out contrasts of shape and texture – rounded, ribbed, feathered, felted, or glossy and smooth. This enormous planning task needs to be undertaken twice a year, for the Potager is replanted in March and again in June. The harvest is so varied that almost every kind of vegetable is grown here, from the humble cabbage to the more exotic ruby chard, and is so abundant that it can truly be called Gargantuan after the legendary giant of Touraine.

The sheer scale of annual work at Villandry is daunting. As well as the planning, 60,000 vegetable plants and 45,000 bedding plants are raised each year to fill the beds in the Potager and ornamental gardens. There are also 140 topiary yews, 1,150 pleached lime trees and 5,000 metres (more than 3 miles) of box hedging to be trimmed and clipped, and 10,000 tulips to be planted; in addition, there are the roses and fruit trees to be pruned. All this is done to exacting standards; the gardens are immaculate.

As a result, every season at Villandry is rewarding. In winter the garden is a graphic pattern of green hedges and black earth, with a tracery of white when frost or snow comes. Spring softens the hard edges with iris, tulips, forget-me-nots and the fresh greens of young vegetable plants; summer sees the Potager and ornamental

ABOVE
In the so-called Deuxième Salon the patterns delineated in box represent music and stylized instruments. The permanent, clipped shapes of the box and yew act as perfect foil to the translucent fleeting quality of the iris flowers.

gardens in their full splendour; and autumn gilds the outline of the lime trees and brings richer colour to vegetables and fruit.

This is a purely formal garden in that it is laid out along perfectly disciplined and geometric lines, but it is quite unlike the formal gardens at Courances, Mormaire or Eyrignac. These rely on grand scale effects – imposing vistas, monumental topiary, classical pavilions or impressive statuary. Instead, Villandry is made up of small-scale ideas writ large – any one of the square vegetable beds or box parterres would convey a comparable effect standing on its own in a small space. In this it looks back to a type of garden that existed before the influence of the Renaissance ideals had been fully felt. Nevertheless, it is the extraordinary scale of Villandry that makes the biggest and most lasting impression.

Villandry needs no advertisement: it has the finest potager in the world and combines two often irreconcilable qualities by being both productive and beautiful.

Structured Informality

In the course of centuries, the art of gardening has moved between two extremes: from the highly architectural designs of Italy and France to the comparative freedom of the landscape and cottage gardens of England. The twentieth century has seen a synthesis of the two traditions: structured layouts tempered by ebullient planting. The device most often and successfully used is a series of enclosures, divided by hedges and generously planted in a variety of schemes.

Part of the popularity of the 'new' style of garden design is due to the ease with which it can be adapted to different sites on quite different scales. Its visual appeal lies in its use of apparently paradoxical elements: the framework provides a reassuring sense of permanence while the limited lifetime of the flowers within conveys a feeling of transience; the controlled outlines are foil to natural planting; and colour and delicacy are intensified by solid green backgrounds.

A good eye for structure and colour, as well as horticultural knowledge, is essential for the creation of successful gardens such as these, which, like Kerdalo, are a reflection of their maker's personality. They convey a sense of understanding between gardener and environment, in the way that nature is both controlled, yet allowed magnificent expression.

In this Ile-de-France garden, the informality of the planting contrasts with structured hedges and symmetrically placed spheres of box. The white garden in late summer includes lupins, foxgloves, roses, artemisia, arum lilies and standard wisterias.

Kerdalo

Prince Wolkonsky's talent as a painter is evident in his sensitive use of colour and the masterly way he groups plants. For the four square beds below the front of the house, he chose a mixture of clear colours toned down with silver-leaved plants, with occasional accents from purple-leaved shrubs. The rose 'Temple Bells' is just starting to climb over the arches in the centre of the lawn. The horizontal tiers of pale foliage of Cornus controversa *'Variegata' appear illuminated against their dark background. The garden building, one of a pair, is gradually being smothered by a climbing rose.*

All the attributes of a great garden are evident at Kerdalo: skilful use of the site, pleasing links with the house, interesting views, subtle colour schemes and unusual plants, all contained within a magnificently planned framework. A strong, masculine garden, it represents twenty-three years of work by the multi-talented Prince Wolkonsky.

He chanced upon Kerdalo when he was on holiday with his children in Brittany. It was an estate of about fourteen hectares (thirty-five acres) consisting, then, of bramble-filled woodland. The large neglected house stood overlooking a valley, while a hill sloped steeply up behind it. Prince Wolkonsky was enchanted by the place. For years he had been labouring over a chalky garden near Paris, where every cartload of soil brought in to improve it seemed to be swallowed up. Meanwhile trips to England had given him dreams of sufficient rain and acid soil for the plants he liked. So it was a delight to find springs, with a brook running down to the river and into a cove near Treguier, as well as the acid soil of this stretch of the French Atlantic coast.

Prince Wolkonsky began by restoring the house, using his skills as architect, painter, sculptor and decorator. He restored the stonework with architectural salvage found in demolition yards, slightly changed the roof angle and moved the building at the right-hand end to produce a well-proportioned house which now gives the impression of both overlooking the garden and enfolding it in its two side wings. He then started work on the garden, making two terraces in front of the house, one below the other, and carving out a series of narrower terraces on the hill behind. The house represents the classic French side of Kerdalo, but the terraces recall Italy, and the choice of plants, as well as their arrangement, are an obvious reminder of England. Kerdalo is a skilful

blend of these three approaches, created in part from the inspiration of gardens visited by the prince during his many journeys abroad – he always carried a notebook to record interesting details – but also by his own intuitive talent.

A walk around the garden begins up on the terraces behind the house. Prince Wolkonsky spent fourteen months with a bulldozer remodelling this area, first digging out more space between the house and the rocky slope looming just behind it, then constructing terraced walks edged with beds of rare plants. These are given structural emphasis by cypress trees, a collection of phormiums with green, purple or variegated foliage which look wonderful in winter – they have managed to survive severe cold – and later interest is provided by bulbs and Mediterranean plants, including cistus, *Convolvulus cneorum*, callistemon, the glaucous spears of

Beschorneria yuccoides, a *Schefflera impressa*, loquat trees and *Echium pininana*.

From here, a path climbs eastwards to a woodland garden, providing a view over a wooden Chinese pagoda designed by Prince Wolkonsky and an architect friend. The pagoda dominates a long canal edged with pale yellow rhododendrons – hybrid *R.* 'Katharine Fortescue' and *R.* Hawk 'Crest' – and, from its position straddling a brook, looks down on two mounds of small-leaved mauve rhododendrons. On the slope behind are massed groups of species rhododendrons with remarkable foliage: *Rhododendron sinogrande*, *R. falconeri*, *R. f. eximium* and *R. macabeanum*, all of which have large leaves with fawn or greyish undersides.

The path takes you gradually down into woodland, 'where you feel the spring more intensely than anywhere else', according to one of the prince's cousins. Everything

PREVIOUS PAGES
Dominated by the Chamaecyparis lawsoniana *'Fletcheri' on the right, this intricately-planted garden picture looks decorative throughout the year. Pink London pride and blue* Salvia × superba *grow among agapanthus on the right; grey* Stachys byzantina *and* Juniperus squamata *'Blue Star' on the left lead to a flush of pale yellow santolina flowers that enliven the dark foliage of* Berberis *'Atropurpurea Nana' which, in turn, contrasts in shape and colour with the* Lychnis coronaria alba.

LEFT
A path leads from the area with the four square

flowerbeds to a broad pool blue mop-head hydrangeas admire their reflections in the water. Earlier in the year, the banks of the pool are golden with Mollis azaleas. The seamlessly woven pattern of the trees – which were all planted by Prince Wolkonsky – draws the eye deep into the dappled woodland beyond.

RIGHT ABOVE
Hazy clouds of amelanchier blossom contrast with fleshier magnolia blooms and rhododendron flowers in the woodland area.

RIGHT BELOW
Magnolia × soulangeana *'Brozzonii' arches over* Rhododendron angustinii.

here is yellow, pale yellow or off-white mixed with blue: amelanchiers, white magnolias, and masses of mauve *Rhododendron augustinii* which were a gift from Lionel Fortescue from his garden in Devon, are combined with Japanese flowering cherries which were given by the Vicomte de Noailles and Cherry Ingram. A touch of deep red comes from a *Berberis thunbergii atropurpurea*. Prince Wolkonsky never disdains a plant for being common; for him anything beautiful is worth planting. Although the soil was naturally acid, a great deal of extra peat and fertilizer have been dug into this area.

At the top of the valley water has been dammed to make one of the nine small pools that the prince decided to construct at the outset to provide a convenient irrigation system. Lacecap hydrangeas (*H. macrophylla*), agapanthus, hostas and papyrus flourish in the cool, damp atmosphere.

The walk continues along the side of the hill, revealing in close-up a scene which had attracted the eye from some distance. This is deliberate: in winter the cheerful golden corner of the estate is visible from the house. Prince Wolkonsky has grouped a quantity of shrubs and small trees with gold or variegated leaves: *Pittosporum tenuifolium* 'Irene Paterson', *P. t.* 'Golden King', *Prunus laurocerasus* 'Castlewellan', green and gold cypresses, variegated privet, all given vertical emphasis by spectacular narrow columns of *Taxus baccata aurea*. We then emerge into a broad clearing dominated by a number of araucarias

and the bristling, ungainly shapes of some strange Chilean conifers. Close by is a group of *Acer pensylvanicum*, remarkable in winter for its coral-coloured bark.

The path meanders back towards the house, past some native trees with rambler roses – mainly 'Toby Tristram' - twining through their branches, then runs down to the flower garden which Prince Wolkonsky made on the terrace below the house. This charming garden in classical style is separated from the terrace above by a retaining wall against which is a double stairway framing a pool and grotto: the steps, carpeted in *Erigeron karvinskianus* (*E. mucronatus*), lead to four large square beds of shrubs and perennials. In the two far corners of the flower garden, opposite the stairway, stand pavilions built in the same materials as the house, their inner walls encrusted with Italian-inspired patterns of *rocaille*, the joint work of Nicole des Forêts and the owner.

In the four square beds, shrubs are used as focal points: philadelphus, purple berberis, deutzia and abelia. Grouped informally around them are massed perennials such as nepeta, Japanese anemones, phlox, echinops, *Crambe cordifolia*, monkshood and euphorbia. The colour scheme is mainly pink and blue, with discreet touches of yellow and purplish red to set off the softer hues; grey-leaved santolina, sage, *Helichrysum splendidum*, wormwood and other artemisias help to blend the colours together. At the centre of this terrace is an arch covered with the climbing rose 'Temple Bells', which has single white flowers in late summer and flexible stems that lend themselves to training.

Wishing to link the flower garden to the terrace above it, Prince Wolkonsky took the advice of an English friend and, in the lower garden, laid out a chessboard design in alternate squares of grass and pebbles similar to those used immediately in front of the house. The upper terrace is a mass of plants, some in luxuriant mounds, some scrambling up the walls or spilling out across the pebbles and paving. Now in thriving maturity, they soften the edges of the old stonework in a graceful blend of colour. Pink, blue and white come from ceanothus (*C. cyaneus* and *C. impressus*), roses, a *Clematis montana*, the pink blossom of an evergreen *Rhaphiolepis × delacourii* 'Kerdalo', the little white bell-flowers of *Libertia formosa* and crinums.

Leaving the lower flower garden and walking south-west towards the valley,

ABOVE
The grotto is in the lowest part of the garden, beside the river Jaudy. It is reached by diamond-shaped stepping stones that barely emerge from the water. The interior of the grotto is decorated with sea images made of shells. Moisture-loving plants such as gunnera, ligularia and petasites grow happily round the pool.

you come to a wild area of acers, hydrangeas, *Hamamelis mollis* and yellow and salmon-pink Mollis azaleas. There is a pool of water-lilies here, beyond which the wooded valley slopes steeply down into a narrow strip where every tree is colonized by climbing roses, schizophragma or wisteria. They form a vast shady canopy for magnolias, camellias, rhododendrons, banana palms and tree ferns. From here a stream runs down to the river Jaudy, its banks thickly planted with Japanese primulas, astilbes, rodgersia, *Lysichiton camtschatcense* and ligularia.

At the bottom of the valley, Prince Wolkonsky has built a grotto decorated inside with shells and symbols of the sea. It can be reached only by stepping stones inspired by Japanese garden design, and it is surrounded by gunnera and bamboo thickets through which the river can be glimpsed. In the grotto one can smell the salt-laden winds from the sea and hear the bells from the cathedral at Treguier.

Kerdalo is a garden that perfectly matches its site, where man and nature live happily together. With passionate enthusiasm, the owner has used boldness and restraint to create a garden where the different parts combine to make a perfectly integrated whole.

LEFT
A chessboard of turf and pebbles lines either side of the lawn on the lower garden, which is reached from the upper terrace in front of the house by a fine double stone staircase designed by Prince Wolkonsky. The steps are being taken over by Erigeron karvinskianus, which seeds itself in the tiniest crevices. Summer colour in the four square beds comes from pink phlox, grey artemisia and purple berberis. The

yellow flowers belong to the curry plant, Helichrysum italicum.

BELOW
The path between the grotto and its pool and the rest of the garden is fringed with pink candelabra primulas, ferns and the vivid green, fleshy leaves of lysichiton. Later, astilbes will take over the role of the primulas. All these plants enjoy the moist, humus-rich soil.

Near Fontainebleau

Designed entirely by the owners during the last twenty years, this is a very individual and unexpected garden – sometimes purely classical, sometimes wildly informal, always itself. The mistress of the house has applied to it her extraordinarily wide knowledge of garden design: everything that she has learned from great masters – such as her uncle, the Vicomte de Noailles, and her mother, the Duchesse de Mouchy – and from her travels, visiting all the most famous gardens in France and England. But if one had to sum up the three most important ingredients, these would be experience, generosity and wit.

It is in this spirit that the garden gives such a welcoming impression, spilling out on to the road where every passer-by can enjoy it. One wall of the old farmhouse gives directly on to the road and is covered in climbing plants – a carefully trained vine, a honeysuckle and several roses, including 'New Dawn'. At their base the walls are satisfyingly thick with shrubs, a cheerful combination which includes a *Magnolia* × *soulangeana*, *Rosa rugosa*, a solid slab of clipped conifer, *Cornus alba* 'Sibirica', and a variegated holly, all outlined with low box hedging.

Once through the gate, you find yourself in a paved courtyard, completely sheltered and enclosed, where the mistress of the house keeps her collection of tender plants. These are grown in pots and moved into the greenhouse in winter: pungent lemon-scented geraniums, pittosporum, fuchsias, plumbago and oleander give a Mediterranean atmosphere which lifts the spirits on grey days. Here, too, are bulwarks of clipped yew and box, some pruned into magnificent topiary shapes. A swan, affectionately clipped and maintained by the master of the house, has, however, somehow turned into a duck.

From here, three steps between sturdy columns of clipped yew topped with elegant spheres take you up into the main

RIGHT
Three shallow steps lined with Cotoneaster microphyllus cochleatus *and framed by neat spheres of yew on clipped pedestals make an elegant entrance to the garden. The immediate feeling of structure is strengthened by the clipped hedges beyond the lawn, while arching fronds of plumbago in oriental porcelain pots add a lighter, delicate touch.*

LEFT

The design at the front of the house reflects the garden as a whole. The free-shaped planting of Magnolia × soulangeana, *variegated holly, and* Cornus alba 'Elegantissima', *are constrained by a grand column of* Thuja plicata 'Atrovirens' *and a neat box hedge. On the walls a grape vine is trained in rows and, to the left of the gate, the planting is balanced by a mass of Boston ivy confined to a tall column.*

LEFT

A harmonious combination of informal planting with formal touches frames the gateway that divides the courtyard from the main garden. On the left, Rosa 'Roseraie de l'Haÿ' *stands behind a topiary yew, whose shape echoes the clipped yew beyond the gate. To the right, pots of pink oleander and blue plumbago, overwintered under glass, bring seasonal colour to the warm courtyard. Behind the wall, a large catalpa, feathery* Phillyrea latifolia *and the flowers of* Clerondendrum trichotomum *provide contrasting form, foliage and fragrance.*

RIGHT

A catalpa shades the comfortable terrace; terracotta pots on decorative columns frame the doorway to the drawing room, adding a formal note.

ABOVE
In the wild part of the garden a mown path through grass curves between birches. The slender silvery trees against the green produce a light and feathery effect, contrasting with the rest of the garden and recalling the Russian heritage of one of the owners.

OPPOSITE
The informal overflowing shapes of the plants in this border – including purple sage, sedum, alchemilla, blue perovskia, variegated cornus and golden spiraea – contrast well with the solid backdrop of massive topiary yews. Further formality is glimpsed across the half-hidden swimming pool, where a box parterre is centred on an urn.

garden. Until recently, fifteen years' growth of *Cotoneaster microphyllus cochleatus* draped these steps, as at Hidcote, creating a charmingly refined effect. All this was destroyed by an intensely cold winter, but some cautious new growth has appeared and everyone is patiently waiting once more.

At the top of the steps, delightful vistas open up all round an expanse of impeccable lawn. To the left, shrubs form an architectural group round an old stone basin; looking ahead, you can just glimpse the swimming pool through a screen of informal shrubs which grow in front of clipped hedges of yew and *Thuja plicata* 'Atrovirens' pruned into amusing shapes such as a castle complete with battlements and arrowslits. Inside the 'room' made by the hedges and beside the swimming pool is a charming little knot garden with sweet-smelling annual alyssum growing between its scrolls of box.

To the right, the garden comes to an end with a border close to the house. Here is a group of plants designed for year-round interest, as the owners come every weekend and like to have something to see from their drawing room windows. A group of hollies, osmanthus, euonymus, with golden or variegated box, helps to give a permanent, informal structure to this border and there are other plants here which look good in both summer and winter: a choisya, *Rosa nitida* for its flamboyant autumn colouring, lavender, santolina, several kinds of sage, rue with variegated or glaucous blue foliage (*Ruta graveolens*), together with dogwoods for their winter bark.

Behind the swimming pool the garden turns into a tree-planted park, where a path winds through a meadow and then back between birch trees to the house. This produces a most attractive effect, a nostalgic reminder of the Russian origins of one of the owners.

As you walk round the garden, you are constantly greeted by new scenes, and it is the surprise and the variety of these that adds so much to its inherent charm. There is also the appeal of the unexpected in the original ways that natural-looking arrangements are mixed with classical shapes.

Château Gabriel

One might wonder what *haute couture* and the natural world could possibly have in common. Perhaps it is a sense of constant change and renewal, as well as of obedience to the passing seasons? Garden design, like that of clothes, is subject to changing taste. These parallels emerge clearly at Château Gabriel, near Deauville, where couturier Yves Saint Laurent and his business partner, Pierre Bergé, have transferred their mastery of the ephemeral world of fashion into that of gardening. The eclectic blend of styles, quoting from the past but at the same time interpreting ideas for today, reconciles naturalism with sophistication, marries curves with straight lines, and informality with restraint in an atmosphere of studied refinement.

Like many of the properties that make the Deauville region so attractive, Château Gabriel dates from the late nineteenth century. A thirty-two hectare (eighty-acre) estate, it had been abandoned for many years when Yves Saint Laurent and Pierre Bergé bought it. Work began in 1979. It took three years to clear the ground, cut down unhealthy trees, mend fences and remodel the site. In this sense the garden is scarcely past infancy, yet its immaturity is not at all obvious. Hundreds of well-grown trees – thirty, forty and fifty years old – were planted and parts of the estate already look like long-established woodland.

With their knowledge of plants, interest in fine gardens and artistic vision, Saint Laurent and Bergé had a number of clear ideas for different areas: a *jardin de curé* (a traditional neat walled garden of fruit and flowers), a rose garden, masses of lavender, a Japanese garden to commemorate a journey there, and a wild flower meadow or woodland garden. To carry through this enormous undertaking, they commissioned landscape artist Franz Baechler, from the Jacques Bedat design group, to put together the different elements. Having

known both men for years, he was able to understand and interpret their ideas, always working closely with them. The firm of Henri Mestrallet helped carry out the work and, of course, their head gardener, Monsieur Jean, kept an eye on it all. Then the designer Jacques Grange introduced an air of authenticity with garden ornaments of the Napoleon III period: a bridge for the Japanese garden, a decorative kiosk of copper and wrought iron, a stairway leading up to the rose garden and a marble basin for its centre.

The entrance is through a 'Gothick' arch made of wood designed by Baechler, which gives a foretaste of the château's half-timbering in 'Deauville' green and immediately sets the atmosphere. The arch leads into a tunnel of hazel trees, their artless delicacy a delight for visitors in spring; then comes a second arch, this time an imposing crenellated gateway in ancient stone fronted by two magnificent sphinxes, the so-called 'Dames de Boulogne'. Beyond it, a curving path wanders among rhododendrons growing beneath a canopy of fir trees (*Abies nordmanniana* and *A. pinsapo*).

The château comes into view on higher

ground, in a splendid setting of evergreen shrubs. The rhododendrons, *Magnolia grandiflora*, plain and variegated hollies, laurustinus, *Viburnum davidii* and bamboo look good at any time of year; at Christmas the single white flowers of a camellia 'Madame Lourmand' stand out against the dark green background. The entrance courtyard is a sophisticated design of elegant paving surrounded by flowerbeds in frames of carefully clipped box, with mounds of evergreen azalea to give a Japanese effect. A paved path leads up to the outbuildings, past a sweeping 'English' border designed by Louis Benech.

To the left of the château, placed so that it can be viewed from the drawing room windows, lies the rose garden, beautifully laid out in a surprisingly horizontal design of classic formality. You are led there by a series of steps and varied levels, which allow you to look closely at some of the plants on the way and then unexpectedly opens out on to this highly structured garden. The atmosphere of tranquillity and contemplation is enhanced by a curved terrace framed by two *Pyrus salicifolia* 'Pendula', which provides views of most of the garden and parkland, over fields of grazing deer and horses, and beyond these to Deauville, the sea and Le Havre bay. The château itself is fringed with grey-leaved plants to set off the colour of the green woodwork: a standard wisteria, lavender, *Elaeagnus* × *ebbingei* and blue cedars.

Walking downhill across the lawn, you come to an undulating, scented river of 'Hidcote' lavender that sweeps right across the garden and all the way down to the pond and towards the sea. You then come to the Jardin de Curé, which is given structure by the walls of two summer-houses and a pergola. Quantities of mainly grey-leaved plants such as *Phlomis fruticosa*, *Ruta graveolens*, *Convolvulus cneorum*, stachys and santolina are planted here, with sages and aromatic herbs interspersed with tall mulleins, onopordums and cardoons. Cordon-trained apples and pears give a framework of straight lines, while the pergola is counterbalanced on the north side by a slope planted with lavender.

On the right, a gate leads to the secret walled garden, where rare plants can bask within its protection. A touch of exoticism comes with the cycas, palms and daturas growing in pots round a pool full of water-lilies set against one of the walls. All these plants spend the winter in a green-

ABOVE
The spacious entrance courtyard makes excellent use of meticulously clipped evergreens, elaborately-patterned paving and a variety of handsome containers.

OPPOSITE
A long herbaceous border runs beside a paved path looking out over the rose garden. In contrast to most of the garden, this has a classically formal layout: centred on the lead bird bath is a symmetrical pattern of box-edged beds.

OVERLEAF
The pergola is swathed in clematis and climbing roses including 'American Pillar', 'Bobbie James', 'Dorothy Perkins', 'Swan Lake', 'Veilchenblau', Rosa anemoniflora and R. filipes 'Kiftsgate'.

house near the offices and outbuildings.

You come back to the winding lavender border at the point where it runs alongside a low wall overgrown with perfumed plants. This is the Promenade Odorante, a scented walk where roses push their way through lavender, hummocks of thyme and mint, narcissi, pinks and lilies of the valley. Accompanied by their mingled scents, you continue down to a Japanese garden separated from the rest of the park by a curving hedge of tall hornbeams. Water cascades into a little pool full of plants which thrive with wet feet: astilbes, Japanese primulas and a *Gunnera manicata*. In May the banks are a mass of Louisiana and bearded irises, like a river of coloured shot silk. On the lawn are small shrubs twisted and dwarfed in Japanese fashion: acers, *Chamaecyparis lawsoniana* 'Nana Gracilis', an oak-leaved beech, even a cedar whose growth was accidentally stunted in a plant nursery and which now has an intriguingly contorted trunk and branches.

The path follows on through collections of rhododendrons, hydrangeas and Mollis

azaleas and finally down to open parkland. Informality takes over in a meadow studded with poppies, cornflowers and oxeye daisies which runs down to a horse paddock and enclosure for deer. Before circling back to the Gothick arch, you can look through to the left into a wooded area of pines and *Cupressus glabra*, where, even in winter, there are splashes of colour from beech and dogwood. To the right, the park twists round tranquil stretches of water reflecting the skies of Normandy.

This is a garden where everything has been thought out, where – in the words of Pierre Bergé – 'even in the most apparently natural areas, nothing has been left to chance.' The visitor passes with magical smoothness from one to another of a whole series of inner gardens. This well-ordered, or, more accurately, disordered procession of scenes and images provides an aesthetic pleasure to go with all the seasonal delights of flowers and fruit. At Château Gabriel even Douce, the tame deer, benefits from the re-creation of a lost paradise.

OPPOSITE
Accentuated by a recent shower of rain, the soft colours of the stone paving from Burgundy blend perfectly with the brickwork of the pergola.

RIGHT
The fragrance of roses and lavender on one side and aromatic low-growing plants on the wall opposite, accompanies a stroll along the scented walk which leads to the Château. The seat painted Deauville green was based on those in Monet's garden at Giverny.

BELOW
The undulating river of lavender continues its meandering course across the garden.

Domaine de la Rivière

This charming estate is set in the Normandy countryside as one always imagines it, or hears about it in old stories, with fruit trees and hedges, thatched cottages and cows, and the sour-sweet smell of apples everywhere.

You come first to a scattering of the half-timbered cottages typical of Normandy set among green hawthorn hedges, then to the seventeenth-century manor house, once a farm. Nearby are so many outhouses that they seem almost a village in themselves. There are sheds for well-kept and sophisticated garden equipment, a building where apples are still pressed for cider and calvados, a store for the best vintages, and an ancient dovecote; pleasing old stables still house a few horses, and a handsome old-fashioned shippon (a kind of barn without walls) in the courtyard holds manure used to fertilize the garden. Flowers for the house grow in a greenhouse and vegetables come from an immense kitchen garden nearby, while private golf greens extend as far as the edge of the forest in the distance.

The garden exists on two levels – an upper area near the house which is essentially comprised of sweeping lawns and

OPPOSITE
A pair of sumptuous herbaceous borders dominates this part of the garden. In May the white flowers towards the front include Cerastium tomentosum *with its silver leaves, old-fashioned* Dianthus 'Mrs Sinkins' *and violas. Further back are blue* Centurea montana, *the slender spears of tradescantia leaves, deep blue violas and geraniums. Behind them are lupins, and peonies and hollyhocks which are about to flower; in the distance are the orange flowers of an azalea. On the opposite side of a croquet lawn is the mirror image of this border.*

LEFT
The dovecote, which is half-timbered like the other farm buildings, is set on a fine expanse of grass and surrounded by fruit trees – apples on the left and pears on the right. Cytisus battandieri *and a young wisteria are being trained up the walls and* Eremurus himalaicus, *white centaurea and silver-leaved artemisias are growing at their feet.*

two huge borders, and a lower, shady area where there is a more structured layout of grass and beds. Louis Benech, a man with extraordinary talents as architect, gardener and botanist, is in charge of the whole garden, and his skill and sureness of touch are evident everywhere, from the mélange of plants around the buildings and the sumptuous planting of the two borders to the arresting design of the lower garden. The plan for the upper gardens was originally the work of Russell Page; he wanted to interfere as little as possible with the natural environment, so he simply opened out the area round the manor house and created a feeling of space with huge surrounding lawns.

In front of the house a croquet lawn extends between the two herbaceous borders, planned to look attractive all year round. In winter they are planted with masses of pansies, primroses and varieties of daisy. Spring colours are soft greys, whites and blues: silvery grey from the leaves of *Cerastium tomentosum*, with its 'snow' of white flowers; blue from centaurea, forget-me-nots and pansies; white from tulips dotted among the rest. In summer there are all sorts of herbaceous geraniums, phlox, lupins, Japanese anemones, lilies, achillea, sage, gaura, *Verbena bonariensis*, *Rudbeckia nitida*, delphiniums and some roses. So that something is always in flower, a few carefully chosen annuals, such as *Salvia horminum* and *Salvia farinacea*, cleome, cosmos and ageratum are planted too. Thus the borders are brilliant with every possible colour, but at the same time they go very well against the background of this rustic setting – all the greenery, the oak beams, old tiled roofs and stonework.

The old dovecote is also fringed with a flowerbed, here planted chiefly in white to match the fantail pigeons. *Eremurus himalaicus*, *Lilium candidum*, *L. regale*, and white *Centaurea montana* have been set against

BELOW

In this border, seen here in August and on the previous page in May, the designer Louis Benech has used a mixture of annuals and perennials to achieve uninterrupted flowering. The annuals include the rare ageratum 'Tall Blue' on the left, white cosmos, cleomes, snapdragons and China roses. The perennial flowers are Japanese anemones, helenium,

Rudbeckia nitida, yellow helianthus, the white phlox 'Jacqueline Maille' and white Achillea ptarmica 'Boule de Neige' together with a few colourful dahlias.

BOTTOM

The glaucous leaves of Romneya coulteri, white valerian and potted fuchsias hide the base of a Clematis 'Hagley Hybrid' and Rosa 'Pink Cloud'.

OPPOSITE

The mixed border in late summer includes Japanese anemones, white cosmos and nicotiana, pale pink hollyhocks, red dahlias and yellow rudbeckias and helianthus.

good foliage plants such as ferns and artemisias. Planted along the front of the building are *Abutilon vitifolium*, monkshood, columbines, catmint and sweet rocket, and trained to grow up the walls are the yellow flowers and silver foliage of a *Cytisus battandieri* that managed to survive the recent cold winter.

A short flight of steps takes you down across a wooden bridge – which was designed by Louis Benech and made on the spot – and on into his lower garden, which is in a clearing surrounded by trees standing high above a wide variety of azaleas and rhododendrons. As it is a recently made garden, although the outlines are clear, the plants are not yet fully mature. Looking down from the top of the steps, you see the defined shape of a four-leaved clover cut out in smooth green turf. Benech chose this motif because the owners of the estate originally came from Ireland, opting for a four-leafed clover rather than a true shamrock because it fitted the space better. Although the design is patterned and formal, the planting is loose and informal. The beds full of woodland plants may seem at odds with their geometrical setting, but here the paradox between the formal structure and informal planting works well, partly because the scheme is placed in a woodland clearing, but mostly because it has been carried out with the conviction and skill of an inventive and knowledgeable designer.

Most of the plants have been chosen to flower in the summer, specifically July and August, with the exception of a few rhododendrons, the skimmias, halesia and *Cornus florida* and *C. nuttallii*.

Benech's enthusiasm for rare plants means that he knows about their upkeep and where they are likely to look their best. Among the hydrangeas, he admires *H. arborescens*, which develops into spectacular mounds, *HH. paniculata*, *p.* 'Praecox', *p.* 'Tardiva' and *aspera villosa*, but his favourite is the pale pink *H. involucrata* 'Hortensis', with its charming crimped double flowers. There are specimens here, too, of the sweet-scented *Clerodendrum trichotomum*, which was brought through intense winter weather under blankets of straw. Benech also likes *Viburnum plicatum* 'Summer Snowflake', which seems to combine the soft outlines of *V. plicatum* 'Mariesii' with the recurrent flowering of *V. plicatum* 'Nanum Semperflorens', (*V. p.* 'Watanabe'). For a late-flowering magnolia he recommends *M. hypoleuca*. Another

ABOVE
*Delightful plant
associations occur in the
borders that are cut into the
clover-leaf lawn. Here a
mix of yellow and white
woodland plants –*
Verbascum nigrum, *and*
Lilium pyrenaicum *which
Louis Benech raised from
seed,* Euphorbia
polychroma *(syn.* E.
epithymoides*) and white
foxgloves – are seen against
a background of* Cornus
controversa *on the right
and* Cercidiphyllum
japonicum magnificum *on
the left.*

fondness is for the fragrant white *Rho-dodendron viscosum* (in fact an azalea) which blooms late in the year. For scent he recommends sweet-smelling clethra, *Betula lenta*, whose stems smell a bit like camphor, *Nothofagus antarctica* with its balsam-scented leaves, and a group of dwarf rhododendrons (*R. lapponicum* and *R. glaucophyllum*) with aromatic foliage.

In another corner he has a collection of shrubs that bear white berries: *Skimmia japonica* 'Fructu-albo', *Euonymus europaeus* 'Albus', sorbus varieties including *Sorbus hupehensis* and *S. cashmiriana*. The last were grown from seed and have berries which start off white and gradually turn pink. Here, too, are *Ilex glabra* and *Callicarpa japonica* 'Leucocarpa'.

There is a glance of sympathetic recognition, too, at what nature has generously provided here. Benech has enjoyed himself going around woods and hedge-banks on the estate, collecting native wild plants such as ground ivy, loosestrife, soapwort (*Saponaria officinalis*), wood spurge (*Euphorbia amygdaloides*) and stonecrop (*Sedum telephium*), all of which he has used in the garden. He has even planted wild strawberries as ground cover.

The design of the lower garden also includes the 'Moon' and the 'Sun' border. Moonlight is represented by tones of grey, white, blue and black – white, for example, turns up in *Tradescantia* 'Osprey', pale blue in *Campanula lactiflora* and *Veronica gentianoides*, black in *Iris chrysographes*, *Fritillaria*

TOP

The heavy heads of an
Hydrangea paniculata
'Grandiflora' show up
against Rhododendron
ponticum *and the small*
glossy leaves of Azalea
pontica.

ABOVE

The distinctive foliage of
rodgersia makes a
handsome contrast with the
*curling ferns (*Athyrium
filix-femina*) and an edging*
of wild strawberry plants.

ABOVE

The lawn in the lower
garden takes the form of a
clover-leaf. Designed by
Louis Benech, the
somewhat formal outlines
of the beds are foil to the
very informal planting
within them. He has used
plants which all flourish in
acid soils: acers, cornus,
rhododendrons, Hydrangea
paniculata *and* H.
arborescens *'Annabelle'.*
In the foreground are white
Geranium pratense, *and*
some white cleomes.

persica, *Viola* 'Nigra' and *V.* 'Molly San-
derson'. Sunshine is represented by colours
on the opposite side of the spectrum – the
yellows, golds and reds of heleniums and
kniphofias, orange hybrid lilies, copper-
coloured *Rosa foetida* 'Bicolor', the tawny
R. 'Lady Hillingdon', deep red *Cercis
canadensis*, *Cosmos atrosanguineus* and the
hybrid *Crocosmia* 'Solfaterre'.

Perception and scholarship, as well as
many touches of wit, have gone into the
making of this garden. There is a sense of
harmony in the balance between imaginative structural ideas and brilliantly conceived planting. The whole garden is consistent, and it is a perfect reflection of the
refined and subtle aesthetic tastes shared by
both owner and designer.

Le Potager

The setting for the garden of Le Potager is a village like many in the Fontainebleau region; Fleury-en-Bière is a cherished place apparently untouched by modern life. Here you are confronted by an enormous sixteenth-century château and a church spire nearby. The garden has been constructed on the site of the former kitchen garden, or potager, of the château and is enclosed by immensely high walls. Plants and trees form a soberly majestic frame to buildings with centuries of history, blending remarkably well with the ancient stonework.

Even before you have gone through the gate of Le Potager, you feel that something marvellous awaits you: in the lane outside, hostas and ferns flourish in a way that can only indicate skilful planting. You go in with a clear sense of the respect and admiration due to so quiet and beautiful a place, to explore what is undoubtedly a Great Garden, the work of that distinguished lady, the Duchesse de Mouchy.

The Duchess began work on the garden in 1950. She took advice from her brother-in-law, the Vicomte de Noailles, and from a Danish cousin, Mogens Tvede, an architect and landscape designer; but soon developed her own taste and skill, and was able to exercise them for more than thirty years. She died in 1982 but her remarkable talent is writ large in the spirit of this garden she has left behind. Renowned in garden circles, she is considered to have been an incomparable gardener with excellent architectural taste. She knew how to set a scene and could tell at a glance why something did not work and just what would make it work. In short, she was mistress of the grand scale effect.

Once inside the walls, Le Potager reveals itself as a large architectural garden divided into green 'rooms', each of which is the setting for a particular theme. Each has its special character, so that you can wander from one to another, constantly fascinated by different sights. Near the entrance is a

OPPOSITE
Magnificent topiary fleur de lis *parade in front of the house whose walls are host to ivy and* Hydrangea petiolaris. *As the white flowers of the climbing hydrangea fade, the mauve-pink lacecaps of the* Hydrangea aspera villosa *on the right come into flower.*

BELOW
The path from the Jardin des Simples – the herb garden – to the pool runs beside a highly stylized formal garden: its geometric design of different coloured gravels is enclosed by bands of close-mown turf, with two yew obelisks as focal points.

OPPOSITE
Walls of scalloped and buttressed yew enclose the Jardin des Simples, a collection of useful herbs with aromatic flowers or foliage, in a mainly grey-green colour scheme. There is purple sage in the foreground, a clump of yellow-flowered tansy on the right and the foliage of pinks makes a carpet in the middle. Mounds of grey

santolina can be seen further back and four climbing roses on frames give height and structure to the design. Behind the yew hedge and across the lawn is the Duchesse de Mouchy's famous topiary 'confessional box'.

BELOW
Clipped topiary provides a sense of structure and stability throughout the garden. Here specimens of Choisya ternata and box help to buttress the wall while a bignonia brings an unexpected but welcome splash of orange, and the silvery tree trunk lightens what would otherwise have been a dark corner of the garden.

long arched pergola draped with *Robinia pseudoacacia* 'Bessoniana'. On the right, backed by an imposingly high wall, a long herbaceous border full of acanthus, delphiniums and hemerocallis is broken up by buttresses of clipped evergreens; on the left, a little door leads to the house façade, which is covered with *Hydrangea petiolaris* and Virginia creeper. A handsome row of yews cut into fleur-de-lis shapes is lined up in front of the house. Beyond an extensive lawn stands a little structure that the Duchess used to call her 'confessional', its domed roof, door and window all carved out of *Thuja plicata* 'Atrovirens', a shrub which lends itself to topiary.

At the end of the house is a paved garden 'room' dominated by a rare tree, *Albizia julibrissin*, which in summer is covered with feathery pink blossom. Although this is the hardiest variety, it hates the cold and suffered a great deal in recent harsh winters. Beside the wall grows the well known 'Aloha' rose, much praised by the Duchess for its vigorous habit and abundant, fragrant flowers. Through her influence, it has been introduced into many other gardens.

From here a path leads to the herb garden, the Jardin des Simples, reached through scalloped yew topiary. Within this geometrically designed enclosure, a colourful, scented mixture of sage, tansy, lavender, alyssum and pinks is allowed to grow informally. The path then slopes down to yet another garden, from which the château and its towers are seen at their best, reminding one of the way the cathedral of St Louis looms above the Potager du Roy at Versailles. A garden could easily be overwhelmed by such a magnificent backdrop. Here shrubs and trees provide a perfect counterbalance to the stonework all around and the design is so strong that it has no difficulty competing with and complementing the surrounding buildings. A dark mass of yews clipped to diamond points makes a commanding statement

A trumpet vine scrambles round the door of the orangery which looks on to the garden where flowers are grown for the house. This 'working' section of the garden is screened by the hedge in the foreground, which is a tapestry of prunus, box and purple cotoneaster.

BELOW
Among the many flowers grown for cutting is the purple form of Eucomis comosa.

BELOW
Among the many flowers grown for cutting is the purple form of Eucomis comosa.

ABOVE
Although the Koelreuteria paniculata *with its mass of pale yellow blooms is not actually inside her garden, the Duchesse de Mouchy has visually included it by making a gap in the boundary yew hedge and bridging it with a fine wrought iron fence.*

along a path which veers right to an elegant orangery. Below this lies a garden where flowers for cutting are grown; it is reached through a tapestry hedge of box, holly, cotoneaster and berberis with a 'door' framed by columns topped with spheres of clipped box.

As you go back to the château, you move down to the right towards a natural-looking pool edged with trees several centuries old and find yourself facing a *trompe l'oeil* statue of a satyr, placed so that it is reflected in the water. It is kept inside during the winter and brought outside on the first fine days of spring. To reach the house again, you walk up over a lawn surrounded by the 'Marie-Jose' dahlias which the Duchess particularly liked for their hardiness and long-flowering quality.

Then comes the Persian Garden designed by the Comtesse de Béhague, who lived in the château during the first quarter of this century. Here the ground is encrusted by a mosaic of porphyry and marble in a design drawn from an ancient Persian document.

Magnolia trees (*M. grandiflora*) were planted here, but some of them have had to be replaced after damage by cold weather.

Finally, surrounded by hedges, there is Saint Antony's Garden, Le Jardin de Saint Antoine, a small enclosure for quiet contemplation, with a bench on which you can rest under hornbeams clipped and shaped to perfection. From here you find that you have come in a circle back to the herb garden. Everywhere you go there is evidence of the creative imagination that went into the making of this garden.

Le Potager went through a very sad phase after the Duchesse de Mouchy's death, but in the last few years it has been taken over and rejuvenated by friends of the family, Monsieur and Madame Behrens. The garden is now well maintained, in keeping with the tastes of its creator. But is it possible to be entirely faithful to the past? As plants grow and develop, gardens must inevitably change somewhat. At Le Potager, however, at least the original spirit remains constant.

Les Trois Pommes

Taking its name from the three apple trees originally in the garden – and the three children in the family – Baron and Baronne de Cabrol's garden near Montfort-l'Amaury in the Ile-de-France has grown over the last forty years to its present state of unity and cohesion. Charming, distinctive, elegant and witty, yet firm and disciplined, are some of the adjectives you might use to describe it.

The most original feature of Les Trois Pommes is the way house and garden are united by the use of severely clipped and trained plants, so that the rigidity of the stone architecture is echoed by equally structured living architecture. The clipped green shapes not only give unity to the whole picture but also stand out against the loose informality of the surrounding planting. Severe outlines contrast with billowing shapes, the dark green of sculpted hedges with the delicate colours of flowers, while a perfectly maintained lawn draws all these elements together.

The de Cabrols bought the eighteenth-century farmhouse in 1949 and, when they renovated the house, turned a decrepit barn at one end into a large drawing room which juts out in such a way that it provides a vantage point over the entire grounds. There are windows on three sides; on one side they open on to the enclosed courtyard near the entrance, on the other to the garden with its view of the countryside and, in the middle, on to a flower-planted area, which links the two parts.

One may wonder how the Cabrols came to achieve such a perfect garden. They admit that there were many uncertainties and mistakes made at the beginning. They subsequently joined the association of Amateurs des Jardins and visited all the finest gardens in England, Ireland, Scotland and Italy. Their close links with the Princesse de Chimay, the Vicomte de Noailles and the Duchesse de Mouchy also

RIGHT
A huge hornbeam arch leads from the garden to a cornfield. Placed so it lines up with the drawing-room windows, it frames the view of the countryside from the house.

OPPOSITE
Monumental clipped evergreens – box, yew and pyracantha – give the garden much of its character and structure. Here they frame and buttress the front of the house and edge a border; on a barn wall, an old and huge pyracantha has been carefully trained and pruned round doors and windows. The solid forms of the evergreens provide a foil for the graceful shape of an old apple tree – one of the trois pommes *of the title.*

RIGHT
Looking back through the massive clipped curve of the hornbeam arch from the fields beyond reveals a glimpse of a cone-shaped yew and low hedge of santolina at the edge of the flower garden.

gave them access to extremely useful advice on gardening aesthetics. The first lesson they learned was to get rid of strong colours, such as red and orange, and the second, as in ordinary life, was to soften any sharp corners. So the garden has acquired a host of clipped, conical yews, some standing guard at the edges of the old barn, near the entrance gate or beside a flight of steps, others at the corners of a formal flower garden, where they are linked by neatly trimmed borders of grey santolina.

The de Cabrols have successfully applied the advice offered by Jacqueline de Chimay which is set out in her influential book, *Plaisirs des Jardins*. In this she says: 'You can

ABOVE

The layout of the flower garden is formal, inspired by old-fashioned potagers. The outline is emphasized by conical yews and clipped edging of santolina, but the controlled architecture of the shrubs contrasts with the informal riot of flowers, including white foxgloves, pale yellow Aquilegia chrysantha, *roses, spires of lupins and delphiniums, and clumps of purple* Salvia × superba.

plant buttresses of clipped box alongside steps without a handrail, or recess doorways in arches of euonymus or yew.'

Entering the courtyard, you are struck by the atmosphere of the garden, the impression that it is looked after and cherished by people of very sure taste. The gate cleverly manages to close itself: the heavy Virginia creeper growing over it has twining stems which hinge it shut behind you. On the left, the garage is walled in pyracantha with neat apertures made for the doors and windows. Above the main flank of pyracantha is an amusing touch – a pair of stag's antlers furred with pyracantha. To the right, a *Cotoneaster horizontalis* has been trained up the house walls to

make an archway round the door; further along an old vine, wisteria, *Jasminum nudiflorum* and an 'Aloha' climbing rose all lay siege to the front of the house.

A short flight of steps beside a rockery massed with spring bulbs takes you down to the lower level of the garden which opens out on to a cornfield through an enormous archway hewn out of hornbeam (which has become increasingly hard to keep in order). It dominates the centre of a long hedge, and has been cunningly placed so that it lines up with one of the glass doors of the drawing room. Finally you come to a flower garden, set out like an old-fashioned potager, its traditional outlines enclosing masses of flourishing shrubs

ABOVE
The view back over the garden from the gentle drifts of colour in the flower garden, across the green expanse of lawn to the mixed borders and orchard beyond, displays a satisfying combination of formal and informal, with the dark clipped yews, in particular, acting as structural punctuation points. It is from the windows on this side of the house that one looks across the garden to the hornbeam arch.

and perennials in a variety of soft colours: sage, campanula, pale blue lupins, delphiniums, white foxgloves, coreopsis, sedums, roses (*Rosa nutkana* 'Plena', syn. *R. californica* 'Plena'), herbaceous geraniums, *Phlomis fruticosa*, poppies, peonies and asters.

The choice of plants in this garden changes from year to year according to evolving tastes, but the basic structure never varies. Flowers may be transient but the trained and clipped evergreen shapes – yew, *Lonicera nitida*, box and small conifers – are unchanging and provide a strong living architectural framework for the garden which suggests a comforting stability and continuity.

A garden in the Ile-de-France

It is amazing to think that an idyllic garden like this exists hidden away to the west of Paris, tucked between an industrial area and a housing estate. Fortunately, it is set in a patch of protected countryside, an island of greenery in urban surroundings, with Versailles and the spire of the village church not far away. The garden, which sits next to a quiet cornfield and a shady strip of woodland, is an exceptionally rich combination of steeply sloping wild garden and an elegantly structured flower garden on some flatter ground below.

The garden has no name but enormous character. It owes this to its creator, who has worked on it for almost two decades with the passion and skill of a painter or musician who also has the technical assurance to enable him to express whatever he wishes.

He bought the land in the protected zone some twenty years ago and built the house, a defiantly modern building, which now overlooks the steeply wooded slopes. When he first arrived this was just a jungle. The ground had to be cleared, brambles torn up and space made round the trees, among which there were some fine oaks and chestnuts well worth reclaiming. The

idea of a garden gradually began to take shape. The owner came originally from the United States of America and from his childhood in New England – where his family had a few hundred acres – remembered his father's idea of making a wild hillside garden; in thinking about the flatter ground, he recalled, too, his father's plans for a flower garden.

He then arranged an analysis of the soil on the slopes below the house. The acidity there meant that he could plant rhododendrons and camellias which grow well in the Ile-de-France, especially *Camellia × williamsii*. So, too, do pieris and interesting varieties of cornus (*C. florida rubra* and *C. kousa*), as well as magnolias and many woodland plants. There are ferns which appear spontaneously, rot down and enrich the soil, Solomon's Seal, primroses and thousands of bulbs. Small rhododendron plants were put in and have grown so well that they now form huge mounds: species rhododendrons were bought from Scotland, as well as azaleodendrons and hybrids such as *Rhododendron* 'Gomer Waterer' whose delicate flowers stand out luminously against the foliage.

As you walk down the path that winds through this woodland part of the garden, you see that here plants seem allowed to grow wild, especially the roses. Ramblers are treated as rough bushes and are left to their own devices; climbing roses find their way up through other shrubs, so you may suddenly see a very double, deep-red rose appearing through the branches of a white rhododendron. Associations like this would be frowned on in a more formal flowerbed, but here anything is allowed and such is the extent to which green dominates the background, everything goes together perfectly.

As you continue down the path, you catch sight of a tall, clipped hedge on the flatter ground below which hints at marvellous things to come. As you get closer,

ABOVE
In the wild part of the garden a lush pool is brightened by the brilliant autumn foliage of liquidambar and Viburnum opulus *shown up against the surrounding green of native trees.*

glimpses of a planned, structured garden beckon you on. A succession of three small green 'rooms' serve as a transition from wild woodland to a more formal garden: the first is bright with plants in pots, the second is a rockery full of alpines, the third a square of beech hedges enclosing a circle of box and a round basin of old stone. The dominant colour of the last 'room' is purple, an excuse for some remarkable audacity on the part of the maker of this garden. He has put together a purple berberis, a mauve *Rhododendron ponticum*, an azaleodendron with young purple shoots and magnificent rose-tinged white flowers and, lastly, the pale apricot-fawn

roses of *R*. 'Buff Beauty'. The basin is lined with acaena and *Mentha requienii* spills over the edges, spreading its scent and seeding itself everywhere. With shadow enhancing all the colours, the beauty of the scene is so intense that you feel compelled to stop to try and take it all in.

You are next led to a long green corridor where a gap in the hedge allows a glimpse of intense blue. This is the first of three flower gardens – blue, white and mauve-pink, each with imaginatively chosen touches of deliberately discordant colour – each of them strictly geometrical in outline, but with plants growing informally in the middle. In midsummer an abundance

of delphiniums dominates the blue garden, their tall stems standing out against the mounds of 'Johnson's Blue' geraniums, chosen to soften the effect. All these blues are pointed up by deliberate contrasts from the yellows of meadow rue (*Thalictrum flavum glaucum*) and Lady's mantle (*Alchemilla mollis*). Early autumn is the time of Michaelmas daisies: *Aster × frikartii* and *A. novi-belgii* 'Professor Anton Kippenberg' appear together with buddleja, monkshood and *Hibiscus syriacus* 'Oiseau Bleu' ('Blue Bird'). The blazing colours of autumn do not seem to reach this part of the garden: summer seems almost everlasting because of the persistent spring-like green from the

ABOVE
Looking down through the wild garden, glimpses of the formal flower garden appear through the branches of autumnal birch trees. The structured layout, enclosed by solid clipped hedges of beech, hornbeam, cypress and yew, makes a striking contrast to the natural woodland.

hedges of Lawson cypress (*Chamaecyparis lawsoniana* 'Green Hedger') in the background.

You next enter the white garden, its outlines indicated only by some clipped spheres of box. Herbaceous peonies, crambe, lupins, hydrangeas, a white mallow, *Lychnis coronaria*, phlox, artemisia, asters, achillea and white valerian (*Centranthus ruber alba*) all blend together beneath the elegant branches of a pair of *Cornus alba*.

Miniature box hedges divide up the mauve-pink garden into a chessboard of flowerbeds, each square containing a mixture of herbaceous plants and roses. They are all there – modern shrubs, English roses

LEFT
The main path from the house to the flower garden winds through the woods which, although left to grow naturally, have been carefully planted. The trees were thinned in places and pockets of fertile soil established for planting rhododendrons and many other acid-loving and woodland plants.

BELOW
The wild garden is particularly lovely early in the year with a profusion of spring-flowering shrubs. In this bright clearing are a white cornus and a pink form, Cornus florida rubra. *Beneath them is a* Rhododendron rubiginosum *with lilac flowers just past their best.*

Between the woods and the maze-like hedges of the flower garden is this attractive rock garden planted on cut slabs of natural stone. Crevices in the stone are occupied by a huge variety of plants: blue aubrieta in the middle, some very fragrant Alpine pinks creeping over the paving, Phlox douglasii from the Rockies, and the starry white flowers of Anemone blanda.

The designer of this garden has shown remarkable control both of large-scale effects and charming small details. Plants deliberately sown in cracks in the paving have subsequently seeded themselves everywhere. Mossy stones provide niches for primrose, Alchemilla mollis, pasque flower (Pulsatilla vulgaris) and white grape hyacinth (Muscari) while later in the year drifts of asters flourish in the background.

From the Lutyens seat at one end of the flower garden is a charming vista through the three garden 'rooms'. The special colour themes are particularly effective seen in succession, from pinks and mauves of the rose garden, to the white garden, and finally the blue garden with its delphiniums. At the end of the vista, the door just off-centre leads to a little pavilion for storing garden tools.

Perennials make delightful company for an old-fashioned rose: deep blue Campanula glomerata mingles with the delicate scented roses of flowering 'Cécile Brunner'.

RIGHT

In summer the profusion of herbaceous plants in the blue garden is at its peak. Shown here are: Campanula glomerata, Geranium × magnificum, *delphiniums and* Iris ensata *(I.* kaempferi*), and, as everywhere in this garden, a particularly effective detail – here a deliberate contrast of colour from some* Achemilla mollis *planted to complement this single-minded blue.*

RIGHT

In the white garden tall spires of lupins make an interesting contrast with the horizontal layers of the overhanging cornus. Their soaring pale shapes are echoed by the foxgloves in the rose garden beyond.

LEFT ABOVE
The entrance to the flower garden offers fascinating contrasts of texture and shape, particularly as the hornbeams – which change with the season – stand beside the evergreen Thuja ocidentalis *'Smaragd'. Their square solidity makes a foil for the delicate feathery mounds of the grass* Pennisetum *flanking the entrance.*

LEFT BELOW
The geometric structure of the rose garden is emphasized more strongly in autumn, when the flat, dark red flowers of Sedum *'Autumn Joy' fill the beds, accompanying fuchsias and the last roses.*

RIGHT
Autumn in the white garden provides a display of fiery red from the cornus and gold from decaying hosta leaves. The framework of the garden, with its hedges and static balls of box, shows up more strongly as winter approaches.

from David Austin – to be enjoyed without prejudice or preconceptions, because of their beauty, scent or ample, healthy growth. *R.* 'Fantin-Latour' has pride of place in front of a Lutyens teak bench and there is a wonderful jumble of 'Reine des Violettes', 'Belle de Crécy', 'Magenta', and 'Tuscany Superb', intermingled with cat-mint, *Stachys macrantha* and a variety of cranesbills (*Geranium psilostemon, G. platy-petalum* and *G. endressii*) joined in September by *Sedum* 'Autumn Joy'.

The three gardens are enclosed by a hedge, with closely planted green and copper-leaved beech, hornbeam, cypress and yew providing a delightful interweaving of colour and texture. Within the gardens there is a constant change of levels and views; steps take you up and down and from one room to another; some of the partitions between the gardens are solid hedges, others built of trelliswork hung with clematis, including the spectacular white 'Marie Boisselot', are designed to be seen through.

The secret of this remarkably consistent garden is the strong underlying structure and the superb handling of plant associations. Contained in such a firm framework, plants can spill out, softening and enriching the overall pattern. They are treated in such a way that it is difficult to distinguish natural effects from those the gardener has contrived: you really cannot tell whether certain things have simply been allowed to happen or made to happen, for example, the fronds of *Geranium endressii* creeping between the slats of a teak bench or the little white pansies seeding themselves in the light green moss between the paving stones. You could spend hours at a time, simply looking, taking in the myriad impressive ideas in this glorious garden.

La Celle-les-Bordes

RIGHT
The view from the main reception room looks over the vast lawn, which was the first part of the garden to be made, and the springboard from which the rest followed. Pots of spiral topiary emphasize the corners of two parterres full of roses.

LEFT
On the left of the huge expanse of grass, the garden rises up towards woodland. The low wall running the length of the garden is broken up by buttresses of box which are foil to a colourful profusion of perennials including saxifrages, Achemilla mollis, *cranesbills and* Cerastium tomentosum, *with taller delphiniums and day-lilies behind.*

OVERLEAF LEFT
Rising up behind the low wall edging the lawn is the woodland garden, which merges into the forest of Rambouillet. Perennial borders gradually give way to evergreens and woodland shrubs such as azaleas, cornus and ferns, which are overhung with the pale slender trunks and delicate foliage of silver birches.

OVERLEAF RIGHT
At the far end of the garden, a crenellated hedge makes a semi-formal boundary between the structured design of the smooth lawn and its colourful surrounding borders and the wild planting and natural growth of the woodland.

An enormous carpet of perfectly smooth lawn extending right to the walls of the early seventeenth-century château is the first view that the visitor has of the garden at La Celle-les-Bordes. Round this lawn lies a garden of great distinction designed by Gilles de Brissac for his parents, the Duc and Duchesse de Brissac. Set on a hillside in the forest of Rambouillet – famous for its stag hunting – it is essentially divided into a sloping woodland area, the lawn, and a more structured, patterned garden.

In fact the garden began when Gilles was still a boy. He had the best possible early training: his maternal grandparents, Monsieur and Madame Eugene Schneider, were passionately interested in the layout of gardens, woods and parkland. They had planted a rose garden round a charming house at Saint-Cloud, which was to be Gilles's home until he was eight. Once the 1939–45 war was over, he spent a large part of his holidays in England, and became fascinated by the villages, the unforced variety and deliberate informality of the garden borders, and the mown lawns.

Influenced by these, he persuaded his mother to make a vast stretch of lawn on the east front of the château at La Celle-les-Bordes. This land had been completely neglected since the time when his great

behind these flourish magnificent clumps of perennials in soft colours – cranesbills, campanulas, thalictrum and day-lilies – while the wall itself makes a home for rock plants such as cerastium, aubrieta, alyssum, iberis and santolina. Breaking up the length of wall into solid slabs of green was the idea of Princesse de Chimay; she had orginally recommended *Lonicera nitida*, but as this needs frequent trimming as well as being vulnerable to frost, Gilles de Brissac decided on box instead, pruning it into the shapes of seats against the wall.

Behind the wall the garden slopes uphill and gradually merges into woodland. This is the wildest part of the garden, where natural vegetation is allowed to develop in almost complete freedom. Hollies and conifers provide a dark green backdrop for the slender silvery trunks of birch, while progressing up the hillside are quantities of Mollis azaleas and *Rhododendron occidentale*, andromedas, camellias, deciduous magnolia, dogwood and broom.

Looking to the right towards the edge of the lawn, the visitor sees a hornbeam hedge pierced with openings like windows which give views over the village and the surrounding countryside. Gilles de Brissac's design was inspired by old drawings of the Trianon Palissade, a green enclosure near the Grand Trianon palace at Versailles in Louis XIV's time. Ingeniously conceived, the arched 'windows' in the hedge are cut at such an oblique angle that viewed from one end of the lawn they appear shut and from the other, open. Below the hedge runs a box border enclosing formal beds of the cluster-flowering rose 'Joseph Guy'.

Lower down, behind the hornbeams, is the swimming pool. It occupies a beautifully sunny position but is quite invisible from the rest of the garden. A high wall on one side provides a delightful foothold between its stones for Mediterranean plants, such as lavender, thyme and creeping rosemary, and for an unusual carpeting dwarf conifer, *Juniperus procumbens* 'Nana'. Clipped yew forms another splendid wall; inspired by an Italian Renaissance garden, it has been trimmed into scroll shapes and given an interesting raised relief pattern.

The sheltered position of La Celle-les-Bordes has allowed Gilles de Brissac to indulge a taste for both formal and wild gardens. The result is an accomplished, elegant blend of freedom and restraint, the epitome of harmonious taste. It is also a marvellous example to any gardener of what patience and persistence can achieve.

grandmother, the Duchesse d'Uzes, had run a stag hunt there, letting her pack of 120 hounds run loose about the estate. The lawn was the springboard from which the rest of the garden slowly took shape. It was the first garden Gilles de Brissac designed and something of a trial run for him, although guidance came from Charles de Noailles and his aunt Jacqueline de Chimay. Today the garden offers the visitor a mellifluous contrast between traditional French formality and a more relaxed English informality.

When you reach the garden through the château's reception rooms – whose walls and ceilings are decorated with 2,400 pairs of antlers – you walk out on to the evenly mown stripes of the huge lawn. From here the view extends into the leafy distance to where massed rhododendrons and Japanese azaleas (red 'Hinode-giri' and pink 'Hinomayo') are interspersed with lily-flowered tulips such as 'West Point', 'White Triumphator' and 'China Pink', daisies and forget-me-nots. On raised ground at the far end of the lawn, spheres of box form an edging in the American manner round a stone basin where a statue of a child holds a dolphin spouting water.

On the left, to the north of the lawn, a long low drystone wall is punctuated by clipped buttresses of box. Between and

ABOVE
Perennials such as lupins and campanulas grow among the roses on the edge of the woodland garden. On the far side of the lawn are more formal beds edged in box in front of the hornbeam hedge.

OPPOSITE
Behind and below the hornbeam hedge is a formal box-edged parterre filled mostly with roses. Growing on the wall to the left are plants that revel in sun and heat: lavender, valerian, iris and santolina. The swimming pool is cleverly screened from view by the beautifully scalloped Renaissance-style yew hedge.

An English Touch

The English approach to gardening, characterized by a particular feeling for generous, informal groupings of plants, has long been admired in France. Several well-known English gardeners have achieved remarkable effects there: Miss K. Lloyd James and Russell Page at Pontrancart, Gertrude Jekyll at Les Moutiers and Penelope Hobhouse at Royaumont. The style has also influenced many French gardeners: the artless charm of English cottage gardens, the atmosphere and colour schemes of Sissinghurst and some of the features of Sheffield Park were the inspiration for Gilles de Brissac's compositions at Apremont.

In every richly-filled herbaceous or mixed border, an English touch is evident; but the profuse, apparently untutored planting is no casual art: to achieve this deliberate blend of texture and colour, with a planned succession of flowering, a close familiarity and deep knowledge of plants is essential. Once learned, the largesse of English planting makes a brilliant marriage with the restrained orderliness of French structure; one shows off the other; there is a tension between the two that unites them and gives them an overall vitality.

The borders at Pontrancart are planted in the purest English manner, the principles of the herbaceous border are faithfully followed in the way that plants are massed in layers and drifts of brilliant, varied colour. The one deviation is that, rather than achieving a succession of colour effects, all the flowers have to be at their peak in late summer. Perennials like valerian, delphiniums and sedum are mixed with annual cosmos, cornflowers and eschscholzia, against a backdrop of shrubs including buddleja.

Apremont

A garden in a village is easily imagined, but a village in a garden is something altogether extraordinary. But this is what Gilles de Brissac has created at Apremont. Here in central France is a garden inspired by an image of English villages, and influenced by the traditional cottage style of garden.

The story began in the early 1930s when Gilles de Brissac's maternal grandfather, Eugène Schneider, having bought all the village houses, proceeded to demolish those which he felt were out of keeping with the medieval or seventeenth- and eighteenth-century buildings. Then, with specialist advice from the architect de Galea, he began rebuilding in the vernacular medieval style. Forty years later, when he inherited Apremont, his grandson found himself in possession of this 'stage' village – its houses with brown roof tiles and façades of warm, peach-coloured stone from the local quarries – but without a suitable green setting. Childhood holidays in rural England had left Gilles de Brissac with memories of Kent and the Cotswolds, of cottages smothered in honeysuckle, clematis and roses, with borders full of lavender, irises and hollyhocks. He decided that he would like to transplant these ideas to France and make a new garden around and among the existing houses.

Vita Sackville-West's white garden at Sissinghurst in Kent was another source of inspiration. At Apremont this idea has been adapted to the local climate and conditions, using plants which grow happily here in the heart of France. Another touch was brought about by a visit to Sheffield Park in Sussex, where the arboretum is centred on a series of interconnecting pools. At Apremont Gilles de Brissac set about constructing a similar arrangement, surrounding the pools with conifers and deciduous trees whose height and vigour bring a vivid dimension to this part of the garden. Finally, he felt that the English tradition of opening private gardens to the public, which was almost unheard of in France at that time, was something he would like to follow at Apremont. His own visits to such places had extended his knowledge of plants, and had given him an immense amount of pleasure as well as ideas to think about, so he felt that he would like other people to benefit from the park and from the creative effort that was involved in it. The design for the four hectares (ten acres) of the Parc Floral first began to take shape in 1971. The first visitors walked through the gates six years later.

Immediately inside the garden, you notice a picturesque group of houses which, without being over-prettified, are not unlike those in Marie-Antoinette's hamlet at Versailles. They are all festooned with climbing plants: honeysuckle, clematis and roses such as 'Madame Edouard Herriot', 'Clair Matin', 'New Dawn', 'Phyllis Bide' and 'Albéric Barbier'. Giles de Brissac likes *Clematis montana rubens*, *C.m.* 'Tetrarose' and *C.m. sericea* (*C. spooneri*) among the small-flowered varieties, and for large flowers he uses 'Perle d'Azur', 'The President' and 'W.E. Gladstone' (all blue); 'Marie Boisselot'

('Madame Le Coultre') and 'Miss Bateman' (white); 'Ernest Markham' (red); and the striped 'Docteur Ruppel'.

Turning your back on the village, you look into the white garden, muted and cool with the grey foliage of artemisia, santolina and *Senecio bicolor cineraria* (*Cineraria maritima*). Here the flower performance begins with all the spring bulbs – narcissi, hyacinths and tulips – followed by perennials such as delphiniums, spiraea, goatsbeard (*Aruncus dioicus*), phlox, arums, gauras and Japanese anemones. Among these are roses: 'Grand Nord', 'Candeur' and the invaluable 'Iceberg'. Gilles de Brissac also uses a variety of summer-flowering bulbs like *Eremurus himalaicus*, *Lilium regale*, white agapanthus, crinums and galtonias, together with acidantheras in September. White annuals – cosmos, snapdragons, cleomes, nicotiana and impatiens – ensure a succession of flowers.

You walk on towards the spring border, delightful for its cheerful blend of colour. Massed herbaceous plants give an impression of rustic profusion – a combination of abundance and simplicity. The unpretentious plants used here – lupins, pyrethrum, columbines, poppies, peonies and foxgloves – are clearly at home in this setting.

ABOVE
Vita Sackville-West's white garden at Sissinghurst was the source of inspiration for this lavish, sweeping border. White-flowered plants – mallows, cleomes, galtonias nicotiana, and Rugosa rose 'Blanc Double de Coubert' – mingle with the soft grey foliage of Senecio bicolor cineraria *on the right, artemisias on the left and, at the back on the right, the gigantic, spidery outlines of* Onopordon nervosum *(syn.* O. arabicum*).*

A long pergola walk entices the visitor on. 'Pergolas are not easy,' says Gilles de Brissac. 'Often the flowers are visible only at the top and from the outside.' His first thought was to choose plants with flowers that would hang down through the arches. Three shrubs fulfilled this requirement – *Robinia hispida*, laburnum and wisteria – so he decided to interweave all three in a sort of waltz rhythm. On the first arch he planted Chinese and Japanese wisteria – he is particularly fond of the long racemes of *Wisteria floribunda* 'Macrobotrys'. For the second arch he chose *Robinia hispida* for its delicious pink hanging blossoms. For the third, a yellow *Laburnum × watereri* 'Vossii', and so on. 'Gardening teaches you to be humble: you start off with a brilliant idea but can't always put it into practice,' comments de Brissac. 'I visualized a most effective succession of blossom throughout May. However, this only worked in my imagination. Laburnums absolutely refuse to grow at Apremont: they don't like the climate or the soil. In the end I had to do just what I'd been trying to avoid, and replace them with climbing roses.' He chose 'Mme Grégoire Staechelin', and 'American Pillar' because his Schneider grandmother was very fond of it.

Next comes the summer border, a charming exercise in cottage gardening, where phlox, perovskia, helenium and day-lilies mingle with tall architectural plants such as hollyhocks, grey-leaved *Macleaya cordata* and silvery *Onopordum nervosum* (*O. arabicum*). Pink crinums, *Agapanthus* Headbourne hybrids and lilies are also happy here. These are greedy feeders and receive a regular diet of manure. Repeat-flowering roses complete the picture: rugosa roses with decoratively crimped foliage, such as 'Roseraie de l'Häy' and 'Blanc Double de Coubert', and trustworthy varieties like 'Ulrich Brunner Fils', 'Milrose' and 'La Sevillana'.

The garden leads through woodland on to the cascade of three pools, inspired by Sheffield Park, and a splendid view across to the château and lakes. In spring the woodland is a carpet of bulbs – muscari, camassia, leucojum, chionodoxa, *Hyacinthoides hispanica* (*Scilla campanulata*) – spread over the ground under ornamental apple trees. *Malus toringoides*, in particular, with the brief splendour of its single white flowers, provides one of the garden's great moments.

The visitor comes next to the arboretum where de Brissac has collected some magnificent specimens. For rapid effect, he brought in hundreds of container-grown trees between fifteen and twenty years old: willows, liriodendrons, liquidambars, *Cupressus arizonica bonita* (*C. glabra*), *Quercus palustris*, *Acer pseudoplatanus* 'Brilliantissimum', ginkgo and metasequoia – many with good autumn colouring.

In the tradition of eighteenth-century park design, a Chinese bridge has been installed over one of the cascade's pools as an eye-catcher for visitors. This was based on sketches by Alexandre Serebriakoff, who has also worked for Charles de Beistegui at Groussay. A 'belvedere' is now being built for the far end of the garden, to provide a view down over the château and river. There is also to be a Turkish pavilion apparently floating on one of the lakes.

For five months of the year there is a delightful succession of plants in flower for the visitor at Apremont. It is a place where nature is treated in the English manner, where soft curves and generous planting convey an impression of permanence and abundance. The château looks down over a river lazily winding between sandbanks, and the whole spacious landscape is an inducement to leave the bustle of town life for a few hours of country tranquility.

ABOVE
The summer border, which also owes much to the cottage garden style beloved by the designer, provides a spectacular succession of colour throughout the season. In the foreground, on the left, are orange snapdragons; an enormous clump of pink lavatera in the middle has grey santolina at its feet, and, behind them, is a glorious mixture of phlox, hollyhocks, mullein, blue Salvia × superba, yellow rudbeckias, daisies, plume poppies and perovskia. All the annuals and perennials are planted in groups large enough in scale to suit this massive border.

RIGHT
The rigorously controlled pattern of the hedge helps to draw this magnificent composition together: the château looks over the garden, and beyond to the parkland which is planted with trees that will blaze with colour in the autumn.

Les Moutiers

The garden and parkland surrounding Les Moutiers, a manor house at Varengeville-sur-Mer near Dieppe, is a masterpiece of gentle English effects laid out on a site which slopes down towards the sea. In part it reflects the influences of Edwin Lutyens and Gertrude Jekyll who drew up the original plans for the garden, but it also represents the vision of one man, Guillaume Mallet, who had been inspired by English gardens, especially those he had seen on the Isle of Wight, and who devoted forty years of his life to make the Parc des Moutiers the work of art that it is today.

Born into a wealthy, garden-loving family, Mallet listened and absorbed much talk of gardens, plantings and colour schemes as a child. As he grew up, the idea of making his own garden became increasingly important to him. When the right moment came, he went in search of a large piece of land, preferably beside the sea, where he could apply many of the principles of English gardening. With weather similar to that in England, and the acid soil suitable for the rhododendrons and woodland plants he wanted to grow, Varengeville was the ideal site, and here Mallet bought ten hectares (twenty-five acres) of gently undulating land.

His wife's aunt, a friend of the Mrs Earl who was well-known for hosting London gatherings of 'Arts and Crafts' enthusiasts, recommended the young Edwin Lutyens for the job of drawing up plans for the manor house and, with Gertrude Jekyll, for a garden around the house. Mallet himself laid out the park. An admirer of the landscape paintings of artists such as Gaspard Duguet and Claude Lorraine, and also a collector of Renaissance woven damask, his approach was like that of a painter, and he filled the park with plants and colours taken from antique textiles. His garden notebooks record everything he ordered at that time. Hundreds of plants would arrive, to be dug up again if, when they

flowered, the colour turned out to be wrong. This perfectionism resulted in a masterpiece of subtle colour harmonies and aptly chosen plants. 'Looking after the garden today can be compared to restoring a painting', comments Robert Mallet, Guillaume's grandson.

From the drawing room windows you look out on to a setting clearly conceived as a consistent whole, with its foreground carefully planned to meld into distant views. The house extends all round into open garden 'rooms', defined by walls which also form a wind barrier. The visitor comes in through the white garden, where squares of low box hedging contain rose bushes ('Iceberg', 'Snow Ballet', 'Frau Karl Druschki' and 'Paulii', a favourite of Miss Jekyll's) and plantings of annual cosmos mingling with perennials such as valerian and lamium. The pure white stands out against a dark yew hedge along one side, while *Hydrangea petiolaris* is trained over stone walls along the other.

A doorway leads into the main courtyard. Lutyens had provided a framework consisting of four cypress trees set into

BELOW

The floating outline of one of the maples contributes its subtle tints to the autumn colours. Silhouetted against the sky are the tall shapes of the blue cedars planted by the creator of the park, Guillaume Mallet.

BOTTOM

Against an evergreen backdrop – here of holly – spring brings a symphony of mauve, blue, pink and cream to this part of the park: scillas associate beautifully with the almost luminous flowers of Rhododendron augustinii 'Green Eye'.

elegant paving. Only one remains, the other three having been killed by cold weather. The Mallet family was anxious to reproduce the original effect, but using less vulnerable trees, and although it was difficult to find replacements with similar leaf texture, colour and shape, they eventually chose *Cupressus dupreziana*.

Two mixed borders in the Jekyll manner provide a welcome on the way up to the house. Buttresses of yews are planted at intervals between roses ('Cornelia', 'Felicia', 'Penelope', 'Prosperity' and 'Roseraie de L'Haÿ'), shrubs (buddleja, mahonia, deutzia) and perennials (phlox, Japanese anemones and campanulas). All the colours here are soft, blended together by grey-leaved plants.

The visitor walks to the right of the house under an English-looking pergola, entwined with yet more roses – 'Cécile Brunner', 'Alister Stella Gray', Albéric Barbier' and 'Lykkefund' – above an edging of perennials. It runs alongside the Sundial Garden, carpeted in the blue-greys of lavender, perovskia and rosemary.

Beyond this lies a clearing planted with magnolias of medium height – 'Merrill', 'Leonard Messel', 'George Henry Kern' and 'Wada's Memory', their fragrant, starry blossom a magnificent sight in spring. In summer, borders of lavishly flowering *Hydrangea paniculata* 'Grandiflora' intermingled with the shrub rose 'Penelope', *Polygonum campanulatum* and an erigeron take over the starring role. They bring you on to the former potager, a walled garden where intersecting paths form a cross emphasized by Irish yews. This area is now being planted as a rose garden, the pink brick walls providing a background for climbing roses such as *helenae*, 'Seagull', 'Bobbie James', 'Climbing Paul Lédé' 'The Garland' and 'Meg'. The borders are a medley of David Austin's 'English' roses and white or deep red herbaceous peonies, all growing among grey foliage and pale blue perennials.

In the patis, or meadow, you walk between flourishing shrubs, graceful drifts of *Mahonia* 'Buckland', given to Monsieur Mallet by Lionel Fortescue from his garden in Devon, an *Epimedium perralderianum* with remarkably large evergreen leaves, camellias, pieris, and *Rhododendron augustinii* 'Green Eye', underplanted with bluebells and steely blue dwarf rhododendrons.

From here you walk down to the park which has been carefully planted to create

marvellous configurations and contrasts of
shapes, textures and colours: there are
groups of holm-oak and holly, smooth
rhododendron leaves show up against
feathery Scots pine, and the coral shoots of
pieris seem to light up the entire woodland.
(Pieris 'Forest Flame' have been replaced
over the years by 'Firecrest' because of its
greater resistance to frost.) The background of blue cedars chosen by Guillaume
Mallet leads the eye to the horizon where
sky and sea appear to merge.

Every season in the park has its special
glory: spring is the time for rhododendrons
and Mollis azaleas, summer for species
roses ('Stanwell Perpetual', *R.* × *odorata*
'Mutabilis', *R. glauca*), drifts of *Iris ensata*
and arum lilies. And late summer is the
time for the countless varieties of hydrangea, while autumn brings the brilliant
hues of maple leaves. Plants form splendid
focal compositions, generously massed to
complement the dimensions of the park.
Linking all these are Robinson-style 'wild'
carpets of naturalized narcissi, anemones,
bluebells, primroses and lady's smock.

The Parc des Moutiers is a place to
delight any visitor; no one could come
away, having walked along the winding
paths through the many and varied groups
of trees and shrubs, without feeling re-
freshed. There is a sense of abiding tranquillity here, a feeling that everything is in
its rightful place, even though the seasons
bring continually changing scenes. A place
to fire the imagination, it is full of ideas for
the private gardener – whether of a large
estate or a small backyard – to emulate.

Royaumont

At Royaumont, Nathaniel de Rothschild's country house in the northern part of the Ile-de-France, the three components of a good garden converge perfectly; the natural demands of the site are met, the preferences of the owner are satisfied, and the style of the designer is fully expressed. But Royaumont is also fortunate to have a brilliant head gardener who interpreted, melded and executed the designs and wishes of designer and owner. When Baron de Rothschild decided to restore the gardens at Royaumont, he approached Penelope Hobhouse, the English gardener and garden consultant, for her advice. Her designs typically use subtle combinations of soft vivid colour in a manner reminiscent of Gertrude Jekyll and of the Impressionists, but also with an individual touch very evident in her garden at Tintinhull in Somerset. It was she who introduced the person who was to become Baron de Rothschild's treasured head gardener, an Englishman named James Priest. A master craftsman and talented landscape gardener who had studied horticulture at Kew Gardens, he transformed the plans into glorious reality.

The garden lies in a cool, damp basin in the middle of a forest and has a river infested with marauding coypu running through it. Near what was originally a farm and is now a comfortable country house, there was a woodland garden created by the Baron Elie de Rothschild, which was planted mainly with azaleas and rhododendrons. This has been retained and now also includes a swimming pool. Baron de Rothschild asked Penelope Hobhouse to create a blue border near the turquoise water of the pool. She used a background of silver-leaved shrubs – hippophae, willows such as *Salix helvetica, Elaeagnus commutata* – to smooth the transition between the woodland garden and this concentration of colour, and used grey-leaved plants – *Artemisia* 'Powis Castle' and *A.*

RIGHT

In August the flowers in the blue border near the swimming pool seem to blend with the blue water. In the centre of the foreground is a clump of Hosta sieboldiana *'Frances Williams'; three small blue-flowered caryopteris are on the left, and several specimens of* Hydrangea arborescens *'Annabelle' are flourishing on the right. In the background, from left to right, are grey-leaved* Artemisia ludoviciana, *the mauve flowers of* Aster × frikartii *'Mönch', and some fading* Gypsophila paniculata *(deadheading would cause gaps in the border).* Salvia uliginosa *can be seen in the distance on the left and* Salvia mexicana *on the right. At the side of the pool are pots overflowing with blue* Plumbago capensis.

OPPOSITE

*Stretching down either side of the main central path of the potager are straight borders enclosing, in April, an informal mass of spring flowers in soft tones of pink (*Tulipa *'China Pink'), blue (forget-me-nots), mauve (pansies) and white (*Tulipa *'White Triumphator) interspersed with clumps of greenish-yellow* Euphorbia × martinii. *At the base of the further column, a patch of* Lychnis coronaria *is about to flower, while honeysuckle (*Lonicera japonica *'Halliana') twines through the trelliswork. The young apple trees are being trained as espaliers to emphasize the straight lines of the design.*

ludoviciana latifolia – to form an immediate background to intensify the blue. Twining clematis like the charming *C.* 'Alba Luxurians' are encouraged to scramble through the shrubs, while massed perennials grow in the foreground. In late summer, blue comes from round heads of agapanthus associated with *Aster × frikartii* 'Mönch' and *Salvia uliginosa*, and a few annuals such as *Salvia farinacea* take over from fading perennials. At the end of the border, huge mopheads from a dozen or so *Hydrangea arborescens* 'Annabelle' contribute a pleasing touch of greenish-white. These shrubs also provide a link between herbaceous and heathland plants. Arranged round the swimming pool are antique porcelain pots planted with blue *Plumbago auriculata* (syn. *P. capensis*) and white acidantheras with black centres.

From here you can go into the former kitchen garden enclosed by yew hedges. The classically linear ground plan of small paths running at right angles to a broader

LEFT
Azalea 'Palestrina' growing behind the blue borders near the swimming pool looks almost luminous against its dark green background.

RIGHT
This path in the potager runs at right angles to the one shown on page 100, the old stone table forming a focal point at one of the intersections. The geometric layout of the garden is accentuated by the lines of trelliswork columns, which were locally made from chestnut wood, draped in honeysuckle. In August, as in spring, the borders overflow with shades of blue, pink and white. A clump of Salvia horminum *'Pink Lady' on the left is echoed, on the right, by blue* Salvia patens *and S.* horminum *'Bluebeard', while the foliage of* Alchemilla mollis *on the left is balanced by the flat pink flowerheads of* Sedum spectabile *and a front line of the annual white alyssum 'Little Dorrit' on the right.*

central walk draws the eye towards a canopy of green trees beyond the hedge at the end of the garden, so that the garden feels larger than it actually is. The main path is bordered with espalier-trained apple trees, while at their feet grow annuals such as *Salvia horminum* and *S. patens*. As Baron de Rothschild likes great armfuls of simply arranged flowers in the house, Penelope Hobhouse drew up a long list of flowers useful for cutting for the huge square beds between the paths. Perennials (Michaelmas daisies, columbines, delphiniums, lupins and erigerons), annuals (wallflowers, snapdragons and asters), double herbaceous peonies and roses (pale yellow 'Princess Michael of Kent' and white 'Margaret Merril') are among those used for the many flower arrangements in the house.

The third garden is in the shape of a large rectangle with one of its shorter sides formed by the house and the other three by a majestic dark yew hedge. Baron de Rothschild wanted to renovate the huge mixed border here in an unmistakably English style and asked Penelope Hobhouse to draw up plans which would make it look good from May until the end of summer. Before planting could begin, the soil had to be carefully prepared and a disease infecting certain desirable plants eradicated. Once this was done, James Priest interpreted the plans, and the garden was brought to life in a distinctively English manner.

The vast L-shaped border with its serpentine outline runs in front of the longest hedge; to give a balance and a sense of structure and permanence, its length is planted with regularly spaced robinias. The size of the border dictated proportionally large planting groups; these are sometimes

LEFT
An ancient Acer platanoides *stands in the centre of the lawn in front of the house.*

BELOW
Designed by James Priest, this section of border opposite the house is centred on the Parrotia persica *which is planted just in front of the yew hedge. In the foreground is some mauve-pink* Verbena rigida (V. venosa) *and yellow* Anthemis 'E. C. Buxton'. *Further on, the border is edged with pink* Diascia vigilis (D. elegans), *which is backed by the distinctive heads of* Euphorbia characias wulfenii. *Behind is a wave of white* Nicotiana affinis.

RIGHT
This huge mixed border, designed by Penelope Hobhouse to provide waves of successive interest, is punctuated by robinias planted at regular intervals. In the foreground are shrub roses ('Nathalie Nypels'); pink Lilium speciosum 'Uchida' *makes a bold statement on the right in front of* Eupatorium purpureum. *The withered plumes of* Astilbe taquetii 'Superba' *are almost hiding in a clump of* Campanula 'Loddon Anna', *while 'Pink Endurance' penstemons grow at their feet. In the distance, feathery white* Artemisia lactiflora *can be seen behind white bottlebrush heads of cimicifuga.*

as much as two or three metres long (six or ten feet) to create maximum effect. And the border itself is more then ten metres (forty feet) deep in places. Annuals and perennials grow side by side. Pastel tones are used throughout: pink comes from Japanese anemones, cleomes, penstemons and *Lavatera olbia* 'Barnsley'; blue from perovskias and *Salvia farinacea*; yellow from lavishly flowering anthemis and *Achillea* 'Golden Plate'; and white from gaura, nicotiana and *Osteospermum ecklonis*. Here one can see how Penelope Hobhouse juxtaposes different colours, blending them against the background of the green foliage of a shrub which has finished flowering, such as *Viburnum plicatum* 'Mariesii'. She has also added a sense of adventure with more vulnerable plants like osteospermum, anthemis, *Artemisia arborescens* and the mauve-flowered wallflower

Every year James Priest takes cuttings of the less hardy plants and keeps them in the greenhouse for the winter. He has also continued to revise and replant various areas at Royaumont – always in keeping with its guiding spirit. Indeed, as Baron de Rothschild has said, without James Priest's intuitive understanding of Penelope Hobhouse's work, the garden would not be the plantsman's haven that it is today.

It would be easy to imagine the gardens of Royaumont under English skies, but not only because of its glorious borders; the lush green lawns here could compete with the best to be found in England; and, like many of the gardens there, Royaumont exudes a gentle but memorable charm.

Pontrancart

The garden at Pontrancart is one of the treasures of Normandy. From the windows of the early seventeenth-century château, one looks out over three gardens. Immediately beneath, at the foot of the château and inside the moat, is the decorative pattern of four parterres: intricate scrolls of little box hedges emphasized by grey-leaved plants. To the right, on the site of the former potager, is a summer garden that at first glance appears to be a very French labyrinth of dark yew hedges; but within the enclosures are exuberant borders of flowers that give a distinctly English flavour to the scheme. To the left you can see the extensive water garden, created by Russell Page, which is in complete contrast to the summer garden, but again English in feel: water, curving outlines and massed herbaceous plants blend perfectly into the surrounding landscape of tall trees, meadows and gentle hills.

In this highly structured garden the tapestry parterres, which are laid out in the formal style contemporary with the Louis XIII château, link buildings and terrace walks. The eye is drawn onwards to the summer garden by the flowers planted on the banks of the moats. Beyond a strip of water, an enormous flower border set against a wall is the first intimation of the splendid sights to come. A huge maze of tall yew hedges divides the area into green 'rooms', each of which is dominated by flowers of a single colour, and as you pass through these, you are confronted by one revelation after another.

The garden was made when the father of the present owner bought the château in the 1930s and transformed what had been a utilitarian estate into an ornamental garden. He wanted to establish a formal layout softened by appropriate plants. His aim was to create the effect of mixed borders, so typical of English gardens, standing out against a dark, luxuriant background. For the choice of colour schemes he called on

the talents of an acknowledged English garden expert, Miss K. Lloyd Jones. Without any doubt, the most delightful of the rooms – and the favourite of the creator of this garden – is the blue room with its mixture of *Salvia farinacea*, ageratum, agapanthus, *Stachys byzantina* (syn. *S. lanata*), perovskia, cosmos, phlox and *Thalictrum delavayi* (syn. *T. dipterocarpum*). These delicate, well-grown flowers in subtle associations of muted colour make an enchanting, tranquil setting.

After the death of his father, the present owner took over the garden, at first as a matter of duty, but later with mounting enthusiasm. Increasingly wide experience, together with his own good taste and affection for this exquisite place, has made him an expert. One excellent change has been carried out: Russell Page has set a circular bed of white 'Iceberg' roses wherever there might be jarring effects or colour clashes between adjoining borders. It is not always easy to devise a transition from one 'room' to another, but now everything is smoothly linked.

Because the owner spends only a month or so in the late summer in Normandy, the flowers all have to be in bloom for that

Warm red tones and cooler pastel colours meet in the long border by the wall. On the left, flat heads of Sedum 'Autumn Joy' and dwarf red 'Collerette' dahlias in front of yellow African marigolds are backed by tall dark red dahlias, with bright cosmos peeping over the wall. On the right, deep blue delphiniums spring up over blue and pink cornflowers and pink cleomes.

LEFT
One of the garden 'rooms' is entirely filled with zinnias, again planted with a careful eye to colour effect, as this view along to one corner shows. Deep red and pink tones predominate at the back next to the yew hedge, moving to orange and yellow at the front. All these annuals are of magnificent quality, grown from specially selected seed brought in each year from all over the world, particularly the United States.

short time. They are mainly unusual, refined varieties of annuals, in the most subtle shades, accompanied by just a few herbaceous plants that flower late in the season. Even these are sometimes treated as annuals and planted out afresh every year. A single criterion applies to them all: flowering must occur simultaneously without fail. This aim is achieved through a carefully programmed flowering calendar. Some plants are held back, others hurried on, with everything depending on the date of sowing.

An achievement such as this would be impossible without the collaboration of owner and head gardener. They work in close partnership, carefully going through the annual seed catalogues from France and other countries, looking out fresh varieties, making nursery trials of new plant associations admired in other gardens the previous year. At the height of the flowering period, the owner takes a critical look round to note possible improvements.

The flowers are clearly happy here. They have a rich diet, with additions of manure from the cows to be seen in nearby fields. Deadheading is carried out every day, and the borders are watered with sprinklers which are run until late at night. All this care means that the summer garden is a brilliant sight every year: the dark, structured background, dense and windproof, forming a superb contrast to huge drifts of gloriously coloured flowers.

The water garden gives a quite different effect, merging as it does into the landscape of Normandy, making the most of the natural setting, and using a range of subtly-coloured plants. Russell Page, much sought after in France and responsible for a number of gardens in both Normandy and the south, was commissioned to design it and to select appropriate plants. It is still young and the herbaceous plants need time to settle in and mature in order to produce the intended picture. But there is already a delightfully peaceful atmosphere.

As you go in, a mass of enormous gunnera postpones a full view of the garden. Once round this, you come to a stream which has been dammed to form a pool surrounded by moisture-loving plants: rodgersia, *Darmera peltata* (syn. *Peltiphyllum peltatum*), *Osmunda regalis*, lythrum and *Iris pseudacorus*. Colours here are delicately blended; dominant mauves originally made the effect rather gloomy, but additions of white – white crinums, cimicifuga and *Lysimachia clethroides* – have lightened this. Flowing water and rustling leaves – clumps of grasses are placed so they catch any wind that blows through – make a lively contrast to the more static feeling in the enclosed flower garden.

Pontrancart is a superlatively successful blend of French style and English taste. Enormous persistence, hard work, dedication and skill go into making it a garden of breathtaking beauty – for just four weeks in the year, four weeks of summer perfection. It is an astonishing achievement.

ABOVE
At the foot of the château is one of four seventeenth-century box parterres, planted with santolina, lavender and neatly clipped dwarf pinks. Across the moat and beyond lies the water garden.

RIGHT
The water garden's lush informal planting and design – by Russell Page – is in contrast with the controlled layout of the flower garden. Seen here are blue agapanthus, creamy astilbe, white Lysimachia clethroides *and behind a clump of pink lythrum, with the great circular leaves of* Petasites japonicus giganteus *on the left and the shaggy spears of* Miscanthus sacchariflorus *rising on the right.*

Echoes of Italy

Perhaps it is not surprising that the closer they are to the Mediterranean, the more Italian is the atmosphere of these gardens. But it is not just the quality of light, the heat and the colours of the earth and the sky that recall Italy. The splendour of the Italian Renaissance reappears in the architecture of pavilions and gateways, of steps, statuary and terraces and, as at La Chèvre d'Or, in magnificent vistas of sculptured shrubs. The use of water, too, has Italian resonances – the cool music of fountains and cascades accompanies a stroll through such gardens at the Villa Noailles.

Terraced escarpments – a legacy of former vineyards – the dark soaring shapes of cypresses, the gnarled trunks and shimmering grey foliage of olive trees, and the blues, greens and ochres set off by the silver foliage of sun-loving plants – all contribute to the alchemy. Scent, that most potent ingredient, completes the illusion: as plants release their fragrance against the warmth of pebbles and paving, the Italian ambience becomes almost tangible.

On one of the terraces created by Lawrence Johnston at La Serre de la Madone, an ornamental pool filled with water-lilies leads to a swimming pool in front of an orangery for tender plants. Orange trees in terracotta pots are set out round the pool and an antique statue stands serenely above the water-lilies. Echoes of Italy reverberate everywhere: in olive and eucalyptus trees, in the ornamental urns, and the combination of old stonework with terracotta and curved Southern tiles.

Villa Noailles

This garden 'room' was once completely enclosed by the hedge. The Vicomte de Noailles's sister, Princesse de Ligne, who had a house nearby at Cannes and was also an expert gardener, often gave her brother advice, and she suggested making an opening in the hedge between two cypress trees. This has given a superb view over the hills of Grasse. Arum lilies (Zantedeschia aethiopica), which enjoy having damp feet, are grown in pots round the pool. The water here is a home for Koi carp, said to be very tame, which the Vicomte was one of the first to introduce into France.

The Vicomte de Noailles is a seminal figure in the contemporary history of private gardens in France. He was one of the first and foremost practitioners of gardening as an art. An aesthete and a botanist, he created a beautiful garden at Villa Noailles, near Grasse, which became a reference point and source of inspiration for all who share a passion for gardens. Although he died in 1981, the structure and features of this essentially Italianate garden – with its beautifully conceived vistas, terraces and sculpted hedges, potted plants and use of water – are a monument to his extraordinary talents.

The garden runs along a south-facing hillside, with views across a valley towards distant hills. Olives were once cultivated here and flocks of sheep, on their way to and from the high summer pastures, sheltered in what was the sheepfold. When Charles de Noailles came here, he was immediately attracted by the landscape and the springs which never dry up, even in the hot summers. He acquired the long-abandoned farmhouse in 1936 but did not begin making the garden until after the 1939–45 war. He designed a structured framework round the house, making a series of courtyards and green hedged 'rooms'; he constructed stone stairways to link the existing level walks along the hillside; and he devised delightful surprise features such as seats and statues, shady pergolas, fountains and summerhouses. The planting was varied, but perhaps planned to look its best in the spring when pieris, Judas trees, flowering cherries, magnolias and thousands of narcissi and fritillaries come into bloom.

From the moment you enter the garden you are entranced by the sound of water: the play of fountains, the murmur of channels, the cool splash against stone overgrown with creeping helxine, maidenhair and hart's tongue ferns. Water provides focal points all over the garden,

ABOVE
Much of the sloping hillside of the Villa Noailles is carved into terraces with retaining stone walls linked by steps. This uninterrupted flight leads down to a damper part of the garden where the Vicomte planted a collection of prunus and magnolia trees. The channel which runs down the centre of the steps was designed for wheelbarrow wheels.

LEFT
A cherub and a marble head which spouts water emerge from a thick curtain of Muehlenbeckia complexa.

often recalling Italy in the wall fountains, in pools, a drinking trough, or gushing from a stone head or gargoyle. Pots of flowers, regularly changed so that they always look fresh, are often used in conjunction with water – as they are close to the house and in the main courtyard, where a Florentine garden of pots is set out on a beautiful pattern of cobblestones with three steps leading to a moss-encrusted pool.

The terrace walk leads to features famous throughout the gardening world: the camellia collection, pink and white-flowering Judas trees trained as a pergola, the splendid garden 'room' with walls of box framing tree peonies. The Vicomte de Noailles was almost visionary in his expert use of green architecture – the sumptuously sculpted hedges, the pairs of trees planted

ABOVE
The Vicomte often used plants for architectural effect. The pergola of beautifully trained Judas trees provides a ceiling of pink and white blossom and much-appreciated shade later in the summer. In perfect proportion to the pergola, the fountain draws the eye along the path, giving it a focal point. The pergola is sited in such a way that, seen from above, it seems to extend the terrace, giving the impression that one might have to walk over the pink openwork floor.

to frame vistas, the climber-covered walls – which provides an elegant framework for the garden. He rejuvenated and reshaped the existing two-hundred-year-old box hedges into exquisite sweeping curves. He planted hedges of yew, bay and myrtle both to act as windbreaks and to make garden compartments. He placed seats between box parterres, or at either end of a vista, so the garden could be looked at from different angles. And, to contrast the more disciplined planting, he encouraged the natural growth of shrubs to soften the formal effect – the *Clematis armandii* which suns itself against old stonework and the *Ficus pumila* which colonizes an entire seat.

In the meadow lower down the hillside he created a scene of extraordinary spring delicacy. Drifts of narcissi and fritillaries

thrive under ancient olive trees, and large numbers of waxy pink and white magnolia flowers stand out against a hazy froth of flowering cherries. The magnolias include *M. campbellii*, *M. liliiflora*, *M. denudata*, *M. kobus*, *M. sargentiana* and *M. stellata*. Among the prunus, the most remarkable are *P. sargentii*, *P. serrulata* and *P.* × *subhirtella* 'Autumnalis'.

The Vicomte de Noailles used to employ several gardeners, but would tour the garden every morning between eleven and twelve and loved walking around with other enthusiasts, discussing plants or giving them away. In his time he had considerable influence on his contemporaries, and his advice continues to be read and valued today. His extensive knowledge of plants which thrive in a warm, sunny

A pale stone seat set against a low wall is the perfect place to enjoy the fragrant flowers of a magnificent Clematis armandii. *On the right, the truncated obelisk of box standing on a plinth is a reminder of the classical motifs used throughout the garden.*

Although these box plants were growing here before the Vicomte de Noailles arrived, he took the risk of cutting them right back to rejuvenate and reshape them. His sure touch and discriminating taste are clear in the architectural detail of the topiary: doors, pediments and variations in relief give a distinguished yet light effect to the wall of box. Grey santolina enjoys the warmth of a low stone wall, while a murmuring fountain recalls the water gardens of Italy. This is the beginning of the magnificent terrace of tree peonies seen opposite.

The tree peonies, which flower for a short but memorable time in early May, need protection from wind, draughts and possible frosts. The Vicomte's solution was to give them a screen of yew. It is balanced by a hedge on the other side of the terrace which is also sculpted to allow contrasts of light and shade. Each of this collection of Japanese species shrubs is contained within a diamond pattern of oxalis.

climate, his experience and expertise as a gardener are all in his book on Mediterranean garden plants, *Plantes des Jardins Méditerranéens*.

Although it is not possible to maintain the garden to the exacting standards achieved in the Vicomte's lifetime, the atmosphere, redolent of classical Italy, is still potent. The adroit use of existing terraces, the exploitation of extensive views over the surrounding Mediterranean landscape, the sense of excitement as a corner is turned to reveal another surprise, the superb compositions of stone and vegetation and, above all, the skilful manipulation of water, are all testimony of a master's hand.

At Saint Jean Cap Ferrat

So admirably does the Italian vocabulary of garden design suit this site, that one could easily imagine the garden to be in Italy. Its sheltered position in one of the warmest coves of the French Mediterranean, on the peninsula of Saint Jean Cap Ferrat, means that the climate, too, suggests Italy.

The owners had had a house and swimming pool here for some years and then acquired an adjoining, narrow strip of land that stretches down to a ledge overhanging the sea. Here they built a house for their guests, which is Palladian in inspiration – reflecting their predilection for Italy, designed by André Svetchine. It was Svetchine who advised them to approach Jean Mus to resolve the problem of creating a garden for the new house that would effectively link it to the main building on a different level. The commission was a challenge for the designer; although the surrounding landscape is stunning, the tongue of land slopes steeply and ends with a precipitous drop down to the sea, toppling boulders and the coastguard path which winds in and out of jagged inlets. It was also necessary to conform to local legislation on planning and conservation; since the garden is visible from a great distance in the curve of a wide bay, the basic contours had to be preserved and the original vegetation kept or replaced with other native species.

Mus felt that everything pointed to an Italian layout for the garden. To link the two properties, he cut straight through the hill, making a line of sight between the two houses. Then he used traditional Italian devices to link the two levels, contriving vistas and linear patterns, constructing terraces and steps, and using terracotta pots and cypress trees to provide the vertical element.

The house for guests on the upper level opens on to a terrace which at one end is closed by a loggia projecting over the sea and at the other end leads to a dramatic

OPPOSITE

The magnificent flight of steps and the stretch of green turf which runs parallel to the sea serves as a link between two houses. Aleppo pines tower above a bank covered with flowering plants, which are tolerant of salt spray and dry soil. In the foreground the long pointed leaves of oleanders stand above white Argyranthemum frutescens. *Cascades of pink ivy-leaved pelargoniums and orange gazanias complement the orangey-pink terracotta tiles and pots which line the steps. The cypresses, looking almost as though they might topple into the sea, contribute to the distinctively Italian ambience.*

staircase which sweeps downwards. Wide, tiled steps, their risers covered with creeping verbena, are punctuated with four pairs of containers planted with standard bay trees clipped into mopheads. Ivy-leaved geraniums cascade down the centre of the steps towards a peaceful expanse of emerald-green grass, which in turn leads to the terrace belonging to the main house.

The proximity of the sea is not a problem, as even in stormy weather little salt spray reaches the plants growing in this promontory garden. On the cliff to the north Mus retained the soaring Aleppo pines which had grown there for many years and planted young specimens of the same tree to the south. Sometimes known as 'Jerusalem' pines, these trees feature in many of Mus's designs; he values them for the hazy outline they make, the writhing trunks that come from leaning towards the light, the silvery pink colour of the bark and the perfume of their needles. As well as all this, they offer no objections to dry soil and sea spray.

To make the most of the glorious backdrop of the sea, Mus used a marine colour scheme of blue, green, grey and white for the plants in the garden. In the blue range, he chose agapanthus, light blue *Plumbago auriculata* (syn. *P. capensis*) to grow up the fences and walls, luminous perovskia and, of course, lavender, while the little mauveveined white bells of *Solanum jasminoides* 'Album' look enchanting scrambling over a low wall. Grey called for santolina, cut back before it can flower, all sorts of artemisia, the velvety leaves of *Helichrysum thianschanicum* (*H. lanatum*), and shimmering silver *Convolvulus cneorum*, with its charming white flowers. White is represented by scented jasmine and white ivy-leaved geraniums. Jean Mus always uses a range of different greens, here preferring reliable plants like *Pittosporum tobira nanum*, which is resistant to coastal conditions, and the white-flowered evergreen *Myrtus*

ABOVE
*The recently built paved
terrace of the guest house
allows glorious views over
the Mediterranean.*

LEFT
*Looking up the steps to the
guest house shows just how
every inch of available
earth has been used to grow
flowering plants. The risers
are host to carpeting plants
such as pink verbena,*
Erigeron karvinskianus
(E. mucronatus) *and*
Persicaria capitata
(Polygonum capitatum);
*ivy-leaved pelargoniums
spill over specially designed
containers in the centre; and
the terracotta pots with
standard bay trees are
underplanted with*
Erigeron karvinskianus.

communis tarentina. In front of these, he has
placed *Nandina domestica*, whose foliage
runs through a whole spectrum of colours
during the course of the year. He has also
included one of his favourite plants, *Olearia
traversii*, for its glaucous colour and the
foliage shaped like olive leaves.

Because the owners of the property
wanted a garden full of flowers and colour,
Jean Mus has brought in touches of pink
here and there with *Persicaria capitata (Polygonum capitatum)*, a pink-flowered ground-
cover plant, which spreads rapidly on the
poorest soils, and splashes of yellow with
hemerocallis and *Cassia corymbosa*.

The effect of this combination of plants
is bright, yet harmonious. Shapes and
colours are handled with a sense of balance
and proportion. Set in a formal architectural framework whose antecedents lie in
some of the great terraced gardens of Italy,
the mood of the garden seems to change
with the sea, always offering a magnificent
spectacle, whether smooth or tempestu-
ous, bathed in sea mist or scoured by the
Mistral.

La Chèvre d'Or

Everything in the garden of this typical Provençal farmhouse suggests Italy. The red soil of Biot, cultivated for two thousand years and used to make pottery famous throughout France, brings to mind the ochre tones of Tuscany; everywhere in the garden it enhances the colours of the plants which grow against it. But the hauntingly Italian atmosphere is evoked by much else besides: the firm structural outlines, the architectural framework, the clipped shapes of the evergreens, the tall dark cypresses and stony terraces, a fountain murmuring in a circle of potted plants, orange and lemon trees and aromatic flowers. The whole setting is flooded with light and baked by the summer sun, with the distinctive shrill sound of cicadas and of trickling water in the background.

OPPOSITE

The garden rises in a series of handsome terraces. The sense of grandeur is accentuated by massive cypresses, stone embankments and topiary effects, such as the pyramids on plinths that emerge out of the clipped box hedge.

BELOW

The formal pool below the house is decorated with pots of scented pelargoniums, kumquats and Lilium regale, *and ornamental statuary. The patterned surface of small cobbles, also used elsewhere in the garden, weaves texture and movement into the terrace and steps.*

Even the curious name of the garden has a Latin origin. Madame Champin, who lovingly made the garden, explains that, according to legend, there is supposed to be a golden goat, the *chèvre d'or*, guarding a hidden treasure within the walls of a Roman ruin standing on the opposite side of the road from the farmhouse; anyone touching this treasure is sure to die.

Scent pervades the garden. Plants are chosen for the fragrance of their flowers and foliage: brush them with your fingers and the perfume stays with you for the rest of your visit. Heliotrope, jasmine, lavender, rosemary, mint, camphor, pineapple sage (*Salvia rutilans*), vanilla-scented *Azara microphylla*, the curry plant *Helichrysum italicum* – all these plants are intensely aromatic. Fleur Champin, the Champins' daughter, brings the garden into the house by making her own pot-pourris.

The garden is situated on a hillside and Madame Champin has made use of the existing horizontal terraces, originally made for olive groves. From the house you gradually descend along a succession of levels paved with pebbles set in patterns, from which views over the garden give a sense of space and distance.

Round the basin on the top terrace are pots of flowering plants – kumquats, frangipani and plumbago – which add to the Mediterranean atmosphere. Water is extremely scarce here and all the fountains and pools depend on a recirculating system.

Lower down, a broad shallow pool is surrounded with caladium flowers which peep out over a carpet of helxine. A charming little ficus (*Ficus pumila*), is allowed to creep down the steps to this pool, but has to be cut back hard from time to time.

Beyond this pool stretches a long vista dominated by a sinuous design of box hedges. Rows of citrus trees alternating with ornamental terracotta pots of myrtle

in each semi-circle of box were, until the recent harsh winters, an integral part of the pattern. While the myrtle has been re-placed, the shade from the flanking wall of cypress trees is too dense to allow new citrus trees to flourish. Nevertheless, the different greens – the curlicues of dark green box, the emerald grass pathway, the almost black cypress and the smooth carpet of soft green helxine which grows behind the box – combine to produce a restful, refreshing effect.

Parallel to this on the right, but a little higher up, there is another line of green box, cut into small pyramids on plinths. These draw the eye on towards a path running up the hill between more magni-

ABOVE
Either side of the allée shown opposite, dimpled cushions of helxine undulate behind the sinuous curves of clipped box, which enclose urns of dwarf myrtle.

OPPOSITE
The vista extending from the elegant Italianate pool and fountain is lined with beautifully scalloped box hedges. Seen here, before severe weather destroyed them, are citrus trees alternating with the grand urns of myrtle inside the loops of box.

ficent cypress trees. And further right still, terraces climb up to a less cultivated section of the garden. You go first through a field of agapanthus, with spherical heads of magnificent deep blue, that are grown for cutting; then on into an area of Mediterra-nean woodland full of rare trees and shrubs – all sorts of maples, pines, oaks, (*Quercus ilex, Q. glauca, Q. coccifera*) and eucalyptus (*E. gunnii, E. parviflora, E. pauciflora*).

Hidden away so that one hardly suspects their existence, are two quite different, equally delectable gardens. Beyond the lines of curving and clipped box and up some steps, you come to the first of these, the Jardin de Monsieur. Inspired by a garden which Madame Champin saw in

LEFT
A secret garden near the house is walled with olive trees, clipped to form a beautiful silvery green hedge. A box hedge encloses the trunks of the trees and is sculpted to form elegant curves near the entrance, into which nestle a pair of statues, half-hiding from the outside world. Overlooking the tranquil green 'room', and serving as an ending focal point, is a distant Pinus pinea.

ABOVE
The view from the entrance to the secret garden looks along to the orangery, a handsome classical building decorated with frescoes and housing a collection of tender plants. The architecture of the orangery is perfectly complemented by the restrained clear lines of the garden design.

RIGHT
A simple pergola supports the branches of lemon trees grown as a tunnel along one of the terraces. There are delicious lemons all year round.

Japan, it is centred on a chessboard design of squares of grey santolina and white sand. Close by are some rare specimens of *Acacia riceanam* (syn. *A. verticillata*).

The second of these hidden gardens adjoins the house. In front of an orangery in the form of an Italianate pavilion, which is used for delicate plants and for occasional meals in the shade, extends a rectangular lawn. This is surrounded by a hedge of medium-height box which hides the trunks of silvery, clipped olives. Creating the effect of a large outdoor room with a doorway marked by a pair of statues, this makes an extremely Italian-looking and soberly beautiful garden.

The garden of La Chèvre d'Or is a highly personal piece of work, the fulfilment of Madame Champin's ambition to

ABOVE
A clump of bright echiums and the strongly scented Wisteria sinensis *covering a pergola frame a grassy path lined with the box pyramid hedge seen earlier on page 127.*

OPPOSITE
This modern parterre and its Japan-influenced surround fit perfectly with the classical Italian ambience of the rest of the garden. Cascades of the sweetly scented double white form of Rosa banksia *arch over a chequerboard of clipped santolina and white sand.*

create 'a place apart from the everyday world, a place for enjoying dreams'. It is also a garden of friendship. The English botanist Basil Lang, a friend who lived near Antibes, advised the owners about plants; the Duchesse de Mouchy suggested making plinths for the line of cones of clipped box; the Vicomte de Noailles used to arrive with gifts of advice and a basket of plants; Baronne de Waldner brought scented geraniums; Sir Peter Smithers presented magnolias and peonies – and so it went on, as the garden slowly grew to its present splendour.

Now it has become a garden where you are happy to abandon yourself to scents and shapes, especially those reminiscent of Italy. It has become a miniature world in which you can forget the passage of time.

La Garoupe

The Italianate château and gardens of La Garoupe, on the Cap d'Antibes, have an aura of unfailing grandeur. The magnificence of their setting – the *garrigue* of the Mediterranean landscape behind and the sea in front, constant sunshine, the clear quality of the light and flawless blue of the sky – all combine to give La Garoupe a sense of paradise regained. Even the heraldic motto above the gate seems to suggest that whoever enters La Garoupe will forget the cares of everyday life.

Both the château and the gardens were created by Lord and Lady Aberconway. It was during a visit to the Riviera in the early twentieth century that Lady Aberconway, who created the magnificent gardens at Bodnant in North Wales, fell in love with Cap d'Antibes. She persuaded her husband to buy forty hectares (a hundred acres) of land on the eastern side of the peninsula and from 1907 until her death in 1934 she spent every winter here. Her daughter inherited the property and in 1965 her grandson Antony Norman in turn became the owner. They have continued to maintain and develop the gardens which perfectly complement the astonishing beauty of their surroundings.

The château, of Italian inspiration, has a

LEFT
The garden extends right to the water's edge; and by building out a balustrade and using plants to make a cascade of flowers spilling down to the sea, the glittering Mediterranean becomes an integral part of the composition. Behind are the white flowers of the silver-leaved Convolvulus cneorum, *mauve* Carpobrotus edulis *and the yellow-flowered* Medicago arborea – *a shrub which does not mind very dry soil.*

OPPOSITE
The terrace in front of the house looks down over one of the magnificent Italian-inspired parterres. Cones of box form accents among the greys and mauves of rosemary, santolina and lavender. The balustrade in the foreground is festooned with the orange-flowered creeper, Streptosolen jamesonii. *On the left is a spherical pair of grey* Teucrium fruticans. *Tall, fastigiate cypresses make dark exclamation marks above the curving tops of umbrella pines.*

series of drawing rooms opening into each other to provide an immensely long vista from the orangery at one end to a huge mirror at the other. From these reception rooms views extend in all directions; on one side you look out over the Bay of Nice backed by the snowy summits of the Alpes Maritimes, on the other a rocky inlet runs towards the open sea. A broad stairway flanked by cypress trees takes you by seemingly endless steps down to the shore through a creek and over the rocks.

Against this is set a garden full of contrasts and changes of mood, subtly tied together by sensitive use of the various opportunities offered by the site. The south side of the château opens out on to a terrace planted with orange trees and a night-scented jasmine (*Cestrum nocturnum*), whose flowers open as darkness falls. Surrounding the terrace is a collection of hibiscus, abutilons, abelias and oleanders, with both single and double-flowered daturas in white, yellow (*Datura chlorantha*) and pink (*D. sanguinea*), that remain in the ground throughout the winter.

From here two huge parterres come into view on either side of a central walk; the inspiration for their immaculately executed geometry came from the garden of the Piazza del Popolo in Rome. A circle of box interspersed with box cones forms the centre of a radial pattern of triangles filled with grey santolina, lavender (*Lavandula pinnata*) and rosemary. Regularly trimmed and shaped, so the pattern is always clear, these parterres are one of the treasures of La Garoupe.

The walk continues towards a pergola draped in jasmine, passion flowers, *Solanum crispum* and campsis. This runs alongside a series of green enclosures: one is a cool, white-flowered garden; another contains a swimming pool encircled by well-watered grass and flowerbeds full of arum, myrtle and *Argyranthemum frutescens*; a third is a little *jardin de curé*, where a priest might

ABOVE
A path that leads from the house down to a rocky inlet in the Bay of Nice gives a distant view of the snow-covered Alps. Growing among the clumps of Mediterranean plants on each side of the steps are some ancient cycas. The Aleppo pines and eucalyptus trees help to provide some welcome shade. Further down there is a glimpse of the pink blossom of the Judas trees mingling with silvery olive foliage.

LEFT
Between the pergola and the house, the soft grey foliage of Pyrus salicifolia *'Pendula' tones down a riot of ivy-leaved pelargoniums. Behind them, a pale yellow datura is backed by bougainvillea trained against the wall.*

RIGHT
A lemon tree trained against the house provides fragrant blossom, evergreen leaves and abundant fruit.

take his evening walk to view an astrolabe set in the middle of neat rectangular parterres. In quite another mood is the garden on the other side of the house, made by Antony Norman to celebrate his golden wedding aniversary; here, all in yellow, is a profusion of mimosa, *Phlomis fruticosa*, *Cornus alba* 'Aurea', *Philadelphus coronarius* 'Aureus', *Helianthemum* 'Golden Queen', *Gleditsia triacanthos* 'Sunburst' and Meilland's 'Soleil d'Or' roses.

Another very different garden has been created on the north side of the château which leads down towards the bay. Within a grid of pathways bordered with the gnarled trunks and tousled silvery foliage of ancient olive trees, a succession of waves of blue, pink and white blossom is splashed against blue sky and turquoise sea. Prunus and magnolia (*M. delavayi, M. wilsonii*) are followed by white spiraea, cercis and thousands of blue iris (*Iris germanica*) in the wide borders under the olive trees flanking

ABOVE
The olive trees make a silvery backdrop for the stunning performance of the ancient Judas trees in full flower. The ground at their feet has been colonized by swathes of orange-coloured antholiza.

RIGHT
Part of the garden is criss-crossed with paths edged with ancient olive trees which, unlike those grown for fruit, are left unpruned so the billowing grey leaves make a perfect foil for the framework of black branches. Beneath them are thousands of indigenous irises which give way to carpets of pink cyclamen.

each of the paths. Later in the year the ground is carpeted with pink cyclamen.

The climb back to the château leads to a pair of cycas, rare natives of Madagascar that grow into distinctive clumps of evergreen pinnate leaves rather like those of palm trees. Although they are not hardy, the climate here is so mild that even in winter they can be left in the ground.

Beyond the main garden lies the *garrigue*, a landscape of Provence – rocky scrubland overgrown with cistus, arbutus and small conifers, native aromatic herbs, *Cyclamen hederifolium* and, in spring, naturalized drifts of sweet-smelling white freesias. Occasional umbrella pines make strong statements, their curving tops a contrast to the tall verticals of cypress whose presence is a constant reminder of Italy. In this setting, the garden leaves the visitor with a persistent memory of a place where you seem to step out of the present into an extraordinary self-contained world.

La Serre
de la Madone

Time and a natural growth of lichen and ivy have given the inimitable patina of age to these ghosts of a former existence.

Where there was a vineyard, tiers of terraces – now edged by hedges – extend beneath overhanging pines from the house to the pool. Amid papyrus and water-lilies an antique statue gazes serenely ahead, looking towards the orangery.

Lawrence Johnston – traveller, plant-hunter and the creator of Hidcote Manor Garden in the west of England – was a man whose refined aesthetic sense was matched by his great architectural talent. In the 1920s he began to spend the winters in Menton on the Riviera, and found a house, in the Gorbio valley, overlooking a slope planted with vines and olives. There he created what was to be his winter garden, La Serre de la Madone, and transformed the hillside into a place of enchantment, reminiscent of Italy, that delighted everyone who saw it.

Johnston began by building a series of terraces to retain the earth and planted wind barriers of cypress trees, and Corsican and Aleppo pines; since it was essential to have water for irrigation and to supply the pools and fountains that he envisaged, he constructed huge tanks for collecting rain water; and he enriched the soil with massive additions of manure.

Although it is now sadly neglected, it is clear that the garden was once a masterpiece. From the house, high above a succession of terraces linked by steps, you walk down into cool shade. The Italian

ABOVE
All the paths in the garden have an objective: this walk leads to an old stone basin planted with papyrus and surmounted by a cherub, and then continues on up the hill behind.

LEFT
One of the series of green balconies between the house and the swimming pool gives a view over the two pools below. The overtones of Italy are reinforced by the sombre presence of the tall cypress trees. Despite obvious neglect, a fragile yellow nasturtium has seeded itself among the blanket of ivy covering the steps, and silky blue irises continue to flower.

influence is apparent as soon as you arrive at the orangery which looks like a Roman villa. Stretching out in front is a reflective sheet of water (made into a swimming pool after Johnston's death), with wide paved margins punctuated with dwarf orange trees in pots. Beyond this is another, smaller rectangle of water, its surface covered with lotus and water-lilies and with an antique statue poised above it. On a lower level you find yourself in a leafy 'room' surrounded by tall plane trees where there is a formal French garden dissected by low box hedges enclosing camellias and species tulips. As you go down more steps, paths lead off right and left, to a particular point of interest: a statue, a fountain or a stone-edged pool. Architectural features like these gradually give way to Mediterranean *maquis*, native wild shrubs such as arbutus, coronilla, myrtles and all kinds of cistus, seeding themselves naturally and spreading their delicious scent.

Lawrence Johnston's travels contributed many treasures which he brought back to La Serre de la Madone. From China he collected seed for free-flowering mahonias such as *M. lomariifolia* and *M. duclouxiana*, which have scented flowers, larger and more upright than those of *M. japonica*. These have seeded throughout the gardens. A collection of tree peonies from Japan is used to edge an avenue of olive trees. Their double or semi-double flowers, white, pale pink and deep red, are interspersed with

the single flowers of herbaceous peonies from the Lemoine nurseries in Nancy. He also brought back various wisterias from Japan, including *W. floribunda* 'Violacea Plena', with immense long racemes, and the soft pink *W. floribunda* 'Rosea'.

The superb structure of the garden was foil to Johnston's sumptuous planting schemes and to picture La Serre de la Madone in its heyday, it needs to be imagined in a cloud of mimosa, with *Mahonia lomariifolia*, white and mauve cercis and naturalized *Amaryllis belladonna* growing in profusion, and, hovering above them, the magnificent flowers of *Magnolia campbelli* and *Magnolia liliiflora*, together with daturas (*DD. arborea, sanguinea, suaveolens*) and exuberant clematis such as *C. armandii*.

The site and climate of La Serre de la Madone both imposed restrictions and opened up possibilities for Johnston that made his Mediterranean garden quite different from his English one; yet both are witness to his innovative talents and intuitive understanding of place and atmosphere. Despite being overwhelmed by plants La Serre de la Madone is unmistakeably imbued with his spirit.

145

Le Vignal

For many years the hills round Grasse have been checkered with fields of scented flowers grown for the perfume industry: a patch of lavender or *Rosa* × *centifolia* here, a tiny vineyard there. In these hills, looking out over silvery hummocks of olive trees broken by dark, almost black columns of cypress, stands the Château du Vignal. Strictly speaking, it is not a château; built in the mid-seventeenth century as a coaching inn, it later became a prosperous farmhouse at the centre of its extensive agricultural estate. It was only a few years ago, after the property was acquired by a Dutch garden enthusiast, that the grounds were redesigned by landscape artist Jean Mus. A native of this sunbaked land, his prime objective was to integrate the garden into the surrounding landscape, using native shrubs and aromatic plants, with additional touches to convey a feeling of Tuscany.

Entering through the classical wrought-iron gates, your first sight is of the garden

OPPOSITE
The steps here wind away from the swimming pool through clumps of Bambusa metake *(now correctly* Pseudosasa japonica*) and a pair of cordylines whose spear-like leaves associate well with the foliage of* Pittosporum tobira nanum. *Behind the two trunks is a paler green mound of* Griselinia littoralis. *The presence of cypress and olive trees is a constant reminder of the Mediterranean.*

OVERLEAF
An orchard of olive trees underplanted with a sea of lavender makes a gloriously restrained composition. The colours reverberate: the lavender flowers echo the blue of the sky, and the grey foliage seems more intense under the canopy of silvery olive leaves. Massed like this, these two quintessentially Mediterranean plants express the true spirit of Le Vignal, while the scent from this mantle of blue makes its own contribution to the redolent atmosphere.

LEFT
Terracotta pots containing flourishing specimens of Camellia sasanqua *'Rosea' stand on each side of one of the main doors in the courtyard. The feeling of a leafy green oasis is enhanced by shrouding the walls in Boston ivy.*

leading up to the old house. Here the layout is formal, reminiscent of Italy and very like the design of gardens in front of the prosperous old farmhouses of Aix-en-Provence. Jean Mus has retained the avenue of ancient pollarded plane trees and punctuated these with clipped cones of dark green box. At the end of the drive, you come to a courtyard with an old stone fountain and look up to the Mediterranean curved roof-tiles of the château.

On the other side of the house there are further resonances of Italy in the formal terrace which, at one end, culminates in a semi-circle of fastigiate cypresses that curves behind a statue. Beyond the terrace, the garden looks out over the hills. Here all the lines are, by contrast, winding and informal. The wide lawn is bordered with massed clumps of silver-leaved plants (santolina, rosemary, lavender, *Phlomis fruticosa, Elaeagnus* × *ebbingei*), contrasting with the dark vertical of cypress trees. This is *Cupressus sempervirens*, cultivated since earliest times in the Mediterranean region and ubiquitous on the hills around the château. Impervious to wind and weather, like impregnable battle lines in the landscape, their narrow vertical outlines and dark shadows scarcely move when the Mistral blows. While they appear to stand guard over the countryside, they do indeed help to preserve it for the future, as their roots prevent soil erosion.

On the left, with a view down over Grasse, is the swimming pool, which has been given an exotic setting, with palm trees, corylines and bamboo. There are also some of the designer's favourite pittosporums, especially *P. tobira nanum*, a miniature shrub which forms evergreen domes and is particularly happy in this climate. It is lightly pruned for dense growth. In early summer, the discreet white blooms have a heady scent rather like orange blossom.

Further left is the Provençal garden, a masterpiece of sobriety based on native

plants, particularly olive trees and lavender, with shapes and contours, colours and scents all blending perfectly with the landscape. This combination has produced a beguiling effect, again with overtones of Tuscany.

The subtle references to Italy, the use of indigenous plants and the combination of massed silvery plants shows the influence on Jean Mus of two designers who, among others, he greatly admires: Russell Page and Tobie Loup de Viane. Russell Page may be said to have imported the English gardening style into France, modifying it according to site or weather, softening the straight lines copied from Italy and creating a gentler atmosphere by making use of massed silver- and grey-leaved plants. Tobie Loup de Viane, a southerner like Mus, liked to go plant hunting and was responsible for re-introducing a number of apparently lost species, such as perovskia, which, with his superb colour sense, he

ABOVE
This old stone capital, discovered when the garden was being constructed, has been made into a fountain. It lies to the right of the main avenue (seen opposite). The coolness and splashing water are much enjoyed by the Acer palmatum dissectum *on the left and the* fuchsia 'Riccartonii' *on the right.*

OPPOSITE
The avenue of pollarded planes interspersed with cones of box leads from the handsome wrought-iron gates to the main doors. Inspired by the traditional garden design of old, well-to-do farmhouses near Aix-en-Provence, it is also reminiscent of Italy.

combined beautifully with local plants and shrubs.

The colours of Vignal are those Mus most likes to use: blue, white and grey – the blue of the southern sky, the white foam of the Mediterranean, and the silvery foliage of olive trees, always present in the hills around Nice. Here Mus has set olive trees against lavender planted in massed drifts of soft blue, creating an effective combination of scent and muted colour.

The Italian resonances that greet you in the formal approach to the house are echoed in its courtyard, in the garden's architectural details and cypress-fringed terrace, and in its Mediterranean surroundings. Against the setting of olive and cypress trees, of scented fields and grassland where sheep graze on their way up to summer pastures, Mus has succeeded in creating a garden which is so perfectly in tune with its environment that it seems to have been there for ever.

Orchestrated Nature

Nature remains resolutely natural-looking in these gardens, their beauty seemingly untouched by sophistication or complexity of design. Although just as much effort might have been expended on them as on any formal garden – the contours of the site exploited, the planting carefully thought out – a sense of spontaneity and naturalness is the key to their success. Adherence to this principle takes different forms. At Le Vasterival each gentle curve has been designed to reveal yet another superbly conceived garden picture where the skilful plant associations are the outcome of years of experience. The garden at Cherbourg is also deliberately orchestrated – but to protect a collection of Mediterranean and sub-tropical plants so that they look as though they had always been at home in northern France. This is different again from Gilles Clément's own woodland garden where nature is given a much freer reign and ecology is encouraged to play a significant role. Whatever their approach, the designer's hand is as unobtrusive as possible so that each effect looks as if it had been produced by happy chance.

Near the brook which runs through La Vallée, wild plants thrive among the cultivated ones, most of which are allowed to fend for themselves. Although the mixture of plants looks entirely natural, the gardener's touch is discernible in the gentle way that tones of tangerine and cream have been introduced to enliven the dark setting. Mollis azalea flowers echo the bark of Acer griseum *and a cercidiphyllum contributes its soft dappled outlines.*

Le Vasterival

For painters, it is the marvellous light which draws them to Varengeville-sur-Mer; for gardeners, the climate, which is like a version of Devon. Prince and Princess Sturdza had always loved the countryside round Dieppe and in 1957 decided to settle here. They wanted to create a garden which would blend into the gentle Normandy landscape, reflecting but not constraining the natural setting, and where all the plants would look at home. They were also determined that it should look good all the year round. Their remarkable dream has been magnificently realized.

Essentially, Le Vasterival is a woodland garden of nearly eight hectares (twenty acres) in which the borders, paths and flowerbeds are designed to follow the natural curves and dips of the countryside. The lack of artifice (there is a notable

OPPOSITE
A natural avenue of trees forms an elegant approach to the house. In the beds that border the grassy walk, species rhododendrons and shade-loving plants grow in profusion.

BELOW
Rhododendrons and azaleas bring rich colour to this woodland walk. On one side are two Mollis azaleas against the dark green of a holly; on the other, Rhododendron 'Halopeanum', with pink buds opening to white, is growing next to R. 'Hindode-giri' against the background of a copper beech.

absence of such decorative features as pergolas, urns, statues, formal pools and clipped hedges) shows the extent of Princess Sturdza's devotion to natural beauty.

A garden of this size cannot be made in a day, and it took immense care and persistence to bring it to its present state of maturity. Clearing the ground initially was an enormous task. The soil was poor – a mixture of clay, sand and pebbles. With winds sweeping in from the sea, it was essential to concentrate first on planting windbreaks – holly, Leyland cypress, laurel and Pontic rhododendrons – all of which have given good protection. But at least the climate is mild and there is enough rain to encourage growth.

The garden now follows the rhythm of the seasons, offering something worth seeing on every day of the year. The plan, however, is quite unlike Gertrude Jekyll's conception of a seasonal theme for different areas of the garden. Instead, each border here has something to offer at every stage of the year, with such variety that there is an infinite succession of plants to look at. Planting is on four levels: first, an underplanting of bulbs (snowdrops, crocuses, scillas, fritillaries, narcissi and colchicums) and ground-cover plants (*Cornus canadensis*, epimedium, tiarella, pulmonaria, omphalodes); herbaceous plants provide luxuriant flowers at the next level; then come shrubs – both evergreen and deciduous; and, finally, a protective canopy of trees magnificently varied in foliage, bark, blossom and fruit.

As you go into the garden, you are confronted by informal drifts of wild rhododendrons before coming to a typical Normandy farmhouse whose walls seem to merge almost imperceptibly with a dark yew hedge. In early summer this forms a splendid backcloth for the huge flowers of tree peonies (Professor Saunders' selection) which are underplanted with scillas, tulips, aconites and asters. A path leads down to

RIGHT
Rhododendrons fill the woodland garden in spring. Here R. griffithianium, *the largest-blossomed of the white-flowered species, is surrounded by R.* fastigiaum, *red R. 'Jock' and R. 'Pink Pearl'.*

LEFT
In spring, colour is carefully orchestrated to create harmonious associations, with enough contrast to catch the eye. Here, Solomon's Seal arches over a carpet of bluebells and Astrantia major. *To the left, the deep pink* Rhododendron *'Hindode-giri', to the right, pale and deep yellow azaleas, while in the background* RR. griffithianium *and 'Pink Pearl' can be glimpsed.*

RIGHT
R. ponticum *hybrids, growing in the shade of Corsican pines, shelter this part of the garden. The damp conditions are perfect for* Primula japonica. *Their bright rounded flower heads contrast with the tall spiky clumps of iris foliage and the pointed leaves of variegated hostas. Behind, the broad glossy leaves of R.* crinigerum *almost hide the orange flowers of the azalea 'Glowing Amber'.*

ABOVE
Le Vasterival is a garden for all seasons and, in summer, hydrangeas provide the woodland with form and colour. Here the blue-white flower plates of the lacecap hydrangea lights up the surrounding green, while its rounded foliage contrasts with the spikes of crocosmia and feathery ferns growing at its feet.

LEFT
The flowers of the hydrangea 'Générale Vicomtesse de Vibraye' (Vasterival selection) glow in the dappled sunlight. These are magnificent specimens, propagated by Princess Sturdza from the finest clones, and specially fertilized.

the *sous-bois*, or underwood, where the tall verticals of maritime pines serve to show up the rounded forms of camellias and rhododendrons.

Behind the house a gently sloping lawn leads the eye down to the valley garden, where prunus, magnolia, sorbus, birch and acer stand out above the borders that gradually reveal themselves with each curve in the path. In the valley bottom a profusion of water plants overhangs the stream and the huge indented shapes of *Gunnera manicata* contrast with the spears of *Iris sibirica* and *I. pseudacorus*, fleshy lysichiton and the rounded leaves of *Ligularia dentata* 'Desdemona', *Petasites japonica* and *P. fragrans*. In summer the flowers of *Iris ensata* (syn. *I. Kaempferi*) seem to hang delicately poised above the pink astilbes.

The remarkable qualities of this garden are especially clear in winter: unlike other woodland landscapes, Le Vasterival never seems gloomy at this season. Even though grey tones and winter cold predominate, there is haunting scent from *Mahonia japonica*, *M. × media* 'Charity' and 'Lionel Fortescue', from *Daphne mezereum*, *Corylopsis pauciflora* and piercing wintersweet. Visually it is astonishingly beautiful when the simplest flower shows up against an enhancing background of evergreen trees and shrubs.

Every effect here is carefully thought out; nothing is left to chance. *Crocus tommasinianus*, a number of hellebores (*Helleborus argutifolius*, *HH. foetidus*, *orientalis*, *niger* and *× sternii*), the *carnea* group of ericas, *Camellia japonica*, *C. reticulata* and *C. × williamsii*, *Hamamelis mollis* and *H. × intermedia*, skimmias (including the rare *Skimmia japonica* 'Fructu-albo'), late rhododendrons such as 'Christmas Cheer', *Rhododendron dauricum*, *R. racemosum* or *R. Praecox* – all these plants are set against the unusual bark of birches (*Betula nigra*, *B. albo-sinensis*, *B. papyrifera*) and acers (*Acer griseum*, *A. davidii*, *A. pensylvanicum*).

Early spring is a magical time when the delicate blossom of prunus and malus sets off spectacular magnolia flowers in a haze of toning pinks. When Greta Sturdza planted the rare *Magnolia dawsoniana*, she knew she would have to wait sixteen years for the first bloom, but her patience has been rewarded by flowers of magnificent size and colour. After these come the intense hues of azaleas and rhododendrons: the finest flowers and most refined foliage are undoubtedly those of the species rhododendrons (*R. yakushimanum*, *R. luteum*,

ABOVE
Pleasing contrasts and harmonies of flowers, foliage and form are the result of careful planting. In the Valley Garden, the white panicles of Hydrangea paniculata *'Grandiflora' are surrounded by* Cotinus coggygria *'Royal Purple',* Hosta sieboldiana *'Glauca' and the scarlet flowers and purple foliage of* Lobelia cardinalis.

R. reticulatum) screened by ancient maritime pines.

In summer the emphasis shifts to herbaceous plants, to roses and especially to hydrangeas. In autumn, splashes of purples and mauves from heathers, the flat pink heads of *Sedum* 'Autumn Joy', and the reddish spheres of *Hydrangea serrata* 'Preziosa' all combine with the brilliant tones of acer foliage (*Acer palmatum heptalobum* 'Osakazuki', *A. palmatum* 'Senkaki', *A. p.* 'Chishio Improved'), sorbus berries (*Sorbus hupehensis*, *S. cashmiriana*, *S. scalaris*) and the little crab-apples of *Malus* 'Crittenden' to create a richly glowing palette of colour.

The plants are amazingly diverse but, since most are those which prefer an acid soil, there is nevertheless a sense of harmony and coherence. A woodland garden demands plants that grow naturally and at Le Vasterival most of the two hundred borders contain an immense number of wild flowers such as violets, bluebells, heathers, ferns, foxgloves and Solomon's seal. Princess Sturdza also has fine collections of rare species. But her main concern is for plants which grow well in either

LEFT
Garden delights continue into autumn. Aralia elata, a small tree whose trunk, flowers and deep blue berries provide interest throughout the year, is particularly decorative with its haze of flowers and graceful leaves turning yellow.

BELOW
The feathery pampas grass and the brilliant leaves of Nyssa sinensis arch over two Vasterival selection hydrangeas – one, white, turning pink in autumn, the other a blue variety that turns red – making a perfectly composed autumn picture.

RIGHT
Hamamelis × intermedia *'Diane', seen in its autumn foliage, is underplanted with* Sedum *'Autumn Joy' and white cross-leaved heather (*Erica tetralix*), and balanced by a clump of the tall heather* Erica terminalis stricta. *The autumn colours glow against the background oaks and evergreens, and are echoed by the bronze foliage of the distant* Zelkova serrata.

colour or form. She has some borders where pink or yellow predominate; elsewhere she has experimented with matching or contrasting colour, or with the interplay of different leaf shapes. All the plants look as though they belong here. Greta Sturdza has suggested a sense of profusion with mass planting, while also allowing each plant breathing space to develop naturally.

A great deal of care is taken over planting, in accordance with the traditional English injunction to spend 'a shilling on the plant and ten on the planting'. Each plant is treated with understanding, is cosseted, fed and, if necessary, protected – though for no longer than two years. All of them stay out in the ground during the winter. One of the secrets of the plants'

ABOVE
In winter, the bright fragrant flowers of Hamamelis mollis *shine like jewels against the tracery of bare branches.*

RIGHT
Evergreen foliage plays an important role in the garden throughout the year. Here the variegated spiny leaves of Ilex aquifolium *contrast with the long leathery leaves of an evergreen rhododendron.*

flourishing appearance is the masterly use of mulching. Every autumn tons of compost and a layer of dead leaves and pine needles are spread over the borders. This is a procedure which cannot harm the soil and indeed benefits the garden in every possible way: the plants are fed and at the same time protected against cold and drought. There is never any need to cover vulnerable plants with straw and, even if there is no rain for months, no watering is necessary. Even if weeds were allowed into this garden, they could not grow through the mulch, so borders look clean throughout the year and plants flourish without competition. Once borders are established, they are never dug. Greta Sturdza simply forks them over and the movement of

ABOVE
Colour and contrast of form is displayed in the winter garden as in any season. The upright red stems of Cornus alba *'Sibirica' (C.a. 'Westonbirt') provide a bright focus, offsetting the pastel shades and soft drooping form of deep pink and white clumps of* Helleborus orientalis *(Vasterival selection).*

earthworms through the soil in winter provides natural aeration. She works in the garden throughout the daylight hours, tending her plants with the help of one gardener, occasional trainees and a young disciple who shares her enthusiasm and to whom she has taught everything she can about her gardening techniques and experiences.

Some people regard untouched nature as a garden; others think gardens should improve on nature, in the way that poetry can heighten prose. Le Vasterival lies somewhere between these extremes – a natural-looking garden, but one which, through the visionary zeal of its owner, is imbued through all the seasons with an intensely poetic atmosphere.

In the Gâtinais Forest

In this subtle woodland garden, the essential forest idiom has been preserved but given a domesticated accent and an additional sense of refinement and elegance. It is the product of various influences, including the natural one of the surrounding Forest of Fontainebleau, that of the designers Tobie Loup de Viane and Edouard d'Avdeew and the tastes and ideas of the owners themselves. As a result, the garden is a magical place where, from year to year, there are extraordinary transformations and improvements which leave no trace of what went before but add to the imponderable, enchanting woodland atmosphere.

It was in the 1970s that Monsieur and Madame Pierre-Brossolette bought several plots of land on the edge of a forest in order to build a traditional house and a swimming pool. Madame Pierre-Brossolette then developed a passion for the garden. As a member of several associations, including Amateurs des Jardins and Association des Parcs Botaniques de France, she visited famous gardens, came to know influential gardeners and so found out about the plants that she wanted to grow. She was inspired by advice from the Comte and Comtesse de la Rochefoucauld, who gave her a number of heathers, and met Princess Sturdza on many occasions. She decided that round the house she wanted to plant valerian (*Centranthus ruber*) and grey-leaved plants such as lavender, *Phlomis fruticosa* and *Senecio* 'Sunshine'. Then she discussed these plans with Tobie Loup de Viane, an artist with a taste for refined detail, subtle colour and unusual plants, and asked him to design the planting layout.

He began by covering the walls of the house with a variety of climbers, both delicate and flamboyant; and with lower-growing shrubs which make a welcoming flourish on every side. The north-facing side of the house hosts shade-loving plants such as *Hydrangea petiolaris*, together with *Schizophragma hydrangeoides*, rarely seen in

ABOVE
Native trees frame this view of the house seen across huge borders carpeted with ground-cover plants such as epimedium, rubus and ivy. Though relatively new, the house is covered with climbers and blends into the garden most naturally.

OPPOSITE
A grassy path runs through the garden, between beds thickly planted with low ground cover and acid-loving shrubs, including dogwoods such as Cornus kousa, C. florida rubra *and* C. nuttallii, *all lying under a canopy of native trees. The curving vistas and naturalness of the planting give the magical effect of a series of woodland glades.*

France but looking very healthy here, and the extraordinary leaves of a *Ginkgo biloba* spreading themselves over a chestnut trellis designed by Loup de Viane. Below these is a mixture of azaleas, pieris, camellias, kalmias and *Rhododendron* 'Gomer Waterer', all now forming splendid dark masses which show off the warm stone of the house. The east wall is covered by the enormous leaves of an aristolochia as well as some evergreen hollies to ensure the walls are not bare in winter. Trained along the south wall, behind a bed of valerians and grey-leaved plants, are a number of shrubs including *Magnolia grandiflora*, with its conspicuous glossy leaves, and the contrastingly fragile leaves of *Ampelopsis aconitifolia*. These combine marvellously with wisteria, with roses – 'Albertine', 'Aloha', 'Wedding Day', 'New Dawn' and *R. banksiae* – and with clematis – *C. alpina*, 'Marie Boisselot' and 'Perle d'Azur'.

Blue is Madame Pierre-Brossolette's favourite colour; one looks into the house and finds a predominantly blue colour

LEFT
The trees and shrubs of this winding woodland garden come right up to the house. The evergreen leaves of nothofagus provide year-long interest above a carpet of heathers: the golden foliage (and pink winter flowers) of 'Jacques Brumage' and the little white bells of summer-flowering daboecias. Visible between the tree trunks are the leaves of a variegated euonymous. The house is clothed, from left to right, in the glossy foliage of three evergreen Magnolia grandiflora, *the delicately cut leaves of a small vine (*Ampelopsis aconitifolia*); and two climbing roses – 'New Dawn' and 'Albertine'.*

BELOW
The terrace close to the house ends in a low wall planted round with grey-leaved shrubs such as Senecio 'Sunshine', Phlomis fructicosa, potentillas and pink valerian. Soft evergreen foliage from a clump of nothofagus provides year-round interest. Beyond is a tranquil expanse of closely mown lawn bordered by the woodland garden.

scheme, with touches of pink, mauve and white. Outside, blue is re-echoed wherever possible, again in conjunction with mauve, pink and white: *Clematis* 'Perle d'Azur', 'Johnson's Blue' geraniums, ceanothus, *Buddleja* 'Lochinch', mauve heather, carpets of periwinkle, *Vitex agnus-castus*, the mauve-tinged white flowers of *Rhododendron* 'Gomer Waterer', lavender, plumbago and scented geraniums on the terrace in ornamental Chinese pots.

Tobie Loup de Viane also contributed to the design of the swimming pool area. He designed, and had specially made, a seat of iroko wood to go round a pine tree; he planted dark mounds of box and *Cryptomeria japonica* 'Globosa' in static contrast to the shimmering turquoise water of the pool; and for the woodland area he designed an octagonal wooden pavilion for storing garden tools with a terracotta finial shaped like an acorn.

It was Edouard d'Avdeew, from whose nurseries the Pierre-Brossolettes bought special plants, who thought of setting a low octagon of yew round this pavilion, and of planting tree peonies in the space between pavilion and hedge. But his main task was to expand and improve the links between different areas of the garden. In sympathy with the natural setting, he wanted to retain the sense of a woodland garden and at the same time to open out views into the surrounding forest so there would be no feeling of enclosure. He arranged for the eye to be led into the distance through a succession of 'scenes' like theatre backdrops; he composed vistas and lines of sight; he planted in huge drifts on the scale of a forest landscape. All this helped to create the illusion that there were no fences round the garden and to give the impression that the garden was much bigger, although there had been no increase in actual area. Elsewhere, he got rid of plants which were too common, such as rhus and spirea, retained local trees like Scots pines and oaks, and planted similar but more unusual subjects for their interesting bark (*Betula albo-sinensis septentrionalis*), or for exciting autumn colour (*Cornus florida* and *C. kousa chinensis*). The woodland area he carpeted with ground cover – periwinkle, rubus and ivy – planting them round massed groups of azaleas and rhododendrons.

The plants seem so much at home in this setting that one feels they must always have been there. Edouard d'Avdeew explains why he chose them: 'I was looking

for a completely natural effect. Obviously there are different schools of thought about this, but my view is that you should not try to embroider nature. The human contribution should be scarcely noticeable. The point is just to suggest an atmosphere.' He has also designed a curved teak bench for the formal garden where flowers are grown for cutting. Set slightly apart, and in a quite different style, this small garden has charming scrolls of box and the bench is set back into a shallow alcove in the tall hornbeam hedge.

You sense a taste here for things that are well made, lovingly crafted objects which spring from designers' hands. The floating leaves, soft colour and dappled shadow, and the curving outlines and springy grass contribute to the exquisite woodland composition and the all-pervading sense of haunting tranquillity.

La Vallée

A refuge for the well-known landscape artist Gilles Clément, whose offices are based in one of the busiest parts of Paris, La Vallée is the most natural of all 'natural' gardens. Here the human hand has been so discreet and so sympathetic to the natural environment that there is no obvious boundary between the garden proper and the surrounding meadows and woods.

Shady, and set on a hillside that dips towards a stream at the valley bottom, La Vallée is a garden almost fluid in its layout, and very different from those Gilles Clément designs for clients. He deliberately chose to have no plan, allowing the garden to develop naturally and the elements to fall into place in their own time. In part this is because here, in Creuse, the region where he grew up, he wanted to return to his roots and experiment with ways of

OPPOSITE
Azaleas fit perfectly into the semi-wild woodland edging the lawn. The pastel colours of the evergreen white Japanese azalea 'Palestrina' and the deciduous pink Knap Hill hybrid 'Cecile' stand out beautifully from the surrounding green.

BELOW
In this garden, colour is often used sparingly but effectively. Here the light carpet of Lamium *'Beacon Silver', the sprinkling of* Meconopsis cambrica *and the luminous foliage of two* Acer shirasawanum *'Aureum' (A.japonicum 'Aureum') brighten a shady hillside.*

creating and managing a garden. On a practical level, this made sense since the distance from Paris – the Creuse region is in the centre of France – makes it difficult for him to keep a constant eye on the place: Clément can spend only two or three months of the year at La Vallée. It is expensive to pay for maintenance and he himself did not want to become a slave to gardening, although he spends a week or two tidying things up when necessary, usually in spring and autumn.

Although Clément was not quite sure what he would do with the garden when he started, he is able to look back and see it in retrospect as an organic whole, and to outline a system of general principles on which he runs the garden. First of all, he waters the garden only in exceptional circumstances. Plants must either grow or give up; he waters them when he puts them in and subsequently leaves them to their own devices. This is a risky policy but on the whole it gives results. Lawns as such do not exist, but the grass manages to stay green, moisture from a nearby spring and stream and the shade of tall trees protecting it even during a prolonged drought.

Clément also tries to maintain the eco-logical balance between plant and animal life in the garden, accepting rather than fighting against it. For example, he refuses to use insecticides on the grounds that if you poison an insect, you poison the bird which eats the insect and so interfere with the whole ecological process. For the same reason, he refuses to get rid of snakes since these are eaten by hedgehogs and are also food for the rare short-toed eagle which continues to survive here because of them. Again, he likes to keep patches of stinging nettles as food-plants to encourage caterpil-lars and consequently butterflies. As he says: 'In meadowland it is the diversity of plant species that determines the diver-sity of insects there, and hence of birds as well.' His argument is most convincing.

ABOVE
This natural-looking profusion of plants includes ferns, acers, Thalictrum aquilegiifolium *and pieris, together with* Tellima grandiflora *and* Lamium, *as well as buttercups and spurge.*

LEFT
*A drift of delicate blue columbines (*Aquilegia vulgaris*) makes a fine foil for the more voluptuous flowers and striking foliage of a double peony. In the distance is a flowering spike of* Rheum palmatum.

OPPOSITE
This scene is dominated by the majestic sweep of foliage of Cercidiphyllum japonicum magnificum. *At its feet are moisture-loving meadow plants such as ranunculus and lady ferns (*Athyrium*).*

Another example is the way he has adapted his planting to rodent behaviour, in this case mainly voles. Because they are fond of eating species tulips, he no longer plants any; on the other hand, since the voles dislike alliums, he has put in a variety of these including *Allium christophii* (syn. *A. albopilosum*) and *A. carinatum pulchellum*. The number of voles is kept down by natural means, since they are a favourite prey of owls by night and buzzards by day.

Finally, Clément explains his theory of the 'dynamic garden' as one which comes into being without any sort of advance plan, by the gardener allowing nature to take its course and watching, then responding, to the opportunities offered. As Clément puts it, 'land which is lying fallow is not land which has stopped developing. There are plants that appear of their own accord and can be of use to the gardener. If I see some foxgloves, I leave them to grow. I go round them with the mower providing them with a kind of unofficial flowerbed. I let them grow and set seed, and mow them down when the leaves start to die back. I may find another clump of interesting plants nearby – mulleins (verbascum), for instance. Again, I mow round them and leave them to develop. Groups of flowering plants like these, which of course change from season to season, take turns as focal elements. The only thing you can plan beforehand is a list of self-seeding plants.'

So Gilles Clément gives nature a free hand and remains aware of the possibilities. Among plants which spread by seeding, he recommends foxgloves and mulleins, caper spurge (*Euphorbia lathyrus*), the stonecrop *Sedum telephium* – which comes up everywhere – columbines (*Aquilegia vulgaris*) and the giant hogweed (*Heracleum mantegazzianum*) more than two metres (six feet) high.

The garden is divided into several areas. Along a charming valley and stream grows an army of Japanese candelabra primulas with muted orange flowers which light up the dark woodland covering the north bank. All sorts of ferns flourish here, too, together with a huge clump of *Gunnera manicata* whose leaves look gigantic beside the delicacy of a splendid *Cercidiphyllum japonicum magnificum*. The 'dynamic' success of the valley depends on plants that are willing to seed themselves, Meadowsweet (*Filipendula ulmaria*) and masses of *Darmera peltata* (syn. *Peltiphyllum peltatum*) never fail to appear in summer, accompanied by a

number of plants which prefer acid soil: *Acer griseum*, *Vaccinium corymbosum*, rhododendrons and azaleas.

To the south, on the steep bank sloping down from the house, Gilles Clément has established a more traditional garden, which includes plants such as phormium, ornamental grasses, a *Rheum palmatum*, herbaceous geraniums, eremurus, with trustworthy *Alchemilla mollis* and *Euphorbia cyparissias* for ground cover. He has martagon lilies flourishing in this setting, dozens of little Californian poppies (eschscholzia) a *Rosa* 'Mutabilis' and a host of plants which he weeds when he must.

Finally, there is a kitchen garden with fruit and flowers: this consists of several squares divided by grass paths and arranged around an old stone feeding trough. Tomatoes, salad vegetables, beans and aromatic herbs look and smell most appetizing, and a few flowers are grown here for the house.

Everything has a positive and negative side. This kind of duality is present in Nature: you can have cultivation or wilderness, domestic animals or pests. At La Vallée, by accepting and being sensitive to the two sides of Nature, Gilles Clément can usually turn her disadvantages to his own advantage.

ABOVE
The distinctive outline of Cercidiphyllum japonicum magnificum overlooks a natural stream which runs through the garden. Indigenous plants, especially ferns, grow wild on its banks.

RIGHT
Near the house, the planting is more open and more organized. On either side of the curving path, somewhat more conventionally arranged borders contain neat clumps of flowers. Here restrained colour is provided by irises and by Californian poppies, sown straight into the ground.

Les Grandes Bruyères

The natural lines and generous massed planting that are the hallmarks of this vast garden – almost a park – are in perfect sympathy with its woodland setting. Immense curving borders, densely planted with trees and shrubs to provide a woodland environment, are dominated by heathers – the *bruyères* that give the estate its name.

The story began, strangely enough, in England. 'We were on a visit across the Channel with one of our children and were visiting gardens. That's when we acquired our passion for heathers. It was an absolute revelation.' This is how the Comtesse de la Rochefoucauld describes the origins of her huge garden. She and her husband built their house in the Orléans forest in the early 1970s, using the style typical of the region. If anyone had told them then that they would one day be in charge of a park full of botanical interest covering many acres, they would never have believed it. 'At that time we knew nothing whatever about gardens. . . . We simply thought of laying down a lawn and having one or two herbaceous borders. But the lawn was always horribly matted and rough, and it was all a great disappointment.' Then came the trip to England. 'When I got back I tried to make deliberate groupings of massed heather, as it grew around us in the forest. We then realized that in fact there was a large family of heathers. So that is where it all began. At first we had guidance from Tobie Loup de Viane, who taught us an enormous amount and helped to get us started. After that we went on by ourselves.'

Over the years the Rochefoucaulds became avid gardeners whose interest and experience in heathers led them to become experts in the field. Bernard de la Rochefoucauld has written a book on the subject, *La Bruyère*, in which he explains methods of cultivation and propagation, control of successive flowering, suitable plant associ-

OPPOSITE
Broad pathways wind through what was once natural woodland. Many of the original trees have been retained, including these Scots pines. Shrubs, perennials, ground cover and bulbs have been added to give interest at all levels. A seat invites visitors to enjoy the view.

RIGHT
The spring garden, which is planted with a wide variety of bulbs including scilla, colchicums and montbretias, gives pleasure later in the year when its interesting collection of hydrangeas, including H. paniculata, *come into flower.*

ations and the design of a heather garden making use of all the varied colours. He is also responsible for creating the Fondation des Parcs de France, based on the English National Trust, which aims to preserve great gardens, parks and botanical collections throughout France. At Les Grandes Bruyères he uses heathers in all the most attractive shades from pink to violet, in a subtle spectrum covering amethyst, mauve, lavender, ruby, cerise-pink, crimson, purple and magenta. The middle of winter is flowering time for *Erica carnea* – the 'King George' variety is even ready for Christmas. *E.* × *darleyensis* continues flowering into late spring, followed in the early summer by *E. erigena* and the tree heaths *EE. arborea* and *australis*. In mid summer come the elegant daboecias, with their little mauve or white bells which last until the first frosts. *Erica cinerea* is very reliable in summer, as is *E. vagans*. Last, *Calluna vulgaris* provides a succession of flowers from early autumn to early winter.

ABOVE
The winter garden has a formal design using evergreen plants such as box, heathers, lavender and santolina; it is enclosed by a pergola and has a round pool in the centre. Arbours and statues are placed to entice the eye along different vistas.

LEFT
Blue delphiniums, variegated ivy and Magnolia grandiflora *form a backdrop for one of the garden's many statues.*

OPPOSITE
Vast areas of the garden are planted with heather, both low-growing and tree varieties, under a protective woodland canopy. Here, hazy summer-flowering heather associates with the flat heads of sedum which are waiting to flower.

'Everything went beautifully for about ten years, until 1985, when calamity struck,' explains Madame. 'It was a disastrous winter, with temperatures as low as minus 32°C (–26°F). Practically all the heathers were killed off. It was a tough lesson for us – we lost almost everything, including a magnificent cypress hedge. So many things disappeared. We changed to other plants and tried to forget about heathers. Now we're coming back to them again. It is very difficult to get qualified help, so when you have a big garden you have to have reliable, trustworthy plants. And among all the countless varieties of heather, there are hardy kinds which don't need much upkeep.'

From the first-time visitor's point of view, it is hard to believe that the garden, which is designed essentially in a vast circle round the house, has lost any of its former magnificence. You come first to the Winter Garden, which is arranged in a chessboard pattern of low box hedging enclosing evergreen plants such as heather, lavender

and *Teucrium chamaedrys*. In the middle, pergolas draped in clematis and climbing roses – 'Albertine', 'Paul Noel', 'François Juranville' and 'Souvenir de la Malmaison' – intersect at a round pool in which there is a gently trickling fountain.

Yews with tops clipped into topiary shapes make handsome buttresses alongside a short flight of steps which takes you down to the left into the Woodland Garden. From the steps the house can be seen in the centre of a broad clearing, in the middle of a now splendidly maintained green lawn. There is a generous sense of space and proportion: it is a place where you can breathe freely, where nothing is cramped or crowded. Grassy walks wind gently through a succession of borders in the Woodland Garden where conifers, oaks, maples, magnolias and cornus overhang the heaths and heathers as well as shrubs such as rhododendrons and azaleas, tree heaths, cistus and potentilla. Planted among them are perennial sedums and asters, and a great number of bulbs, including magnificent clumps of crinums and montbretias.

In this part of the garden, the soil is mulched with crushed pine bark and improved with additions of cow manure and a natural, seaweed-based fertilizer. The Comtesse de la Rochefoucauld never uses chemical fertilizers or weedkillers, a principle based on her feeling for nature and ecology. Birds are paramount and even such normally undesirable creatures as wasps, hornets and moles are allowed to live in the garden. Cleopatra the grass snake appears to enjoy the task of eating slugs, so the clumps of hostas here have magnificent, undamaged leaves.

As you walk round you come to the Spring Garden, that part of the Woodland Garden which is carpeted with naturalized bulbs such as muscari, scilla and puschkinia. This, is turn, leads to the Arboretum, an area of over sixteen hectares (forty acres) where every year the Rochefoucaulds plant a hundred or so new subjects, mainly grown from seed. They are trying to acclimatize species from all over the world, particularly America and Japan: liquidambar, taxodium, tsuga, albizzia, zelkova and all sorts of birches with unusual bark. And here, too, there is a special collection of magnolias that look magical in spring.

From here you walk back towards an informal maze, known as The Labyrinth, where clipped hornbeams form green enclosures for old roses, most of them

ABOVE
Near the edge of the formally designed rose garden, roses make an embroidered outline for an imaginary window.

OPPOSITE
Clipped hornbeam makes a handsome boundary between woodland and the more formal area of the garden near the house. These hornbeam hedges curve round the edge of the wild garden which is a satisfying blend of different shapes and shades of green.

grown from cuttings brought from L'Häy-les-Roses. The Comtesse has a passion for collecting old roses and, since for her the scent is the most important feature of any rose, this area is full of perfume from 'Great Maiden's Blush', 'Reine des Violettes', 'Duchesse de Montebello' and 'Petite Orléanaise'.

Walking on you find yourself back at the house again, admiring the way in which the courtyard makes a sympathetic link between the house and the garden. The courtyard was planned by Tobie Loup de Viane, who has, as Madame said, 'such wonderful architectural sense'. It is a beautiful, classically simple design: all round it is a buttressed wall of clipped hornbeams and in the space between each buttress is a *Magnolia grandiflora*.

Gardening here is a passion that devours time. Planned with a generosity of spirit, it is a garden in which the philosophy of its creators can be read: they find great beauty in nature; they respect its laws and intervene as little as possible.

On the Cherbourg Peninsula

The road runs in sweeping zig-zags from high above the coast to the village below. One feels as though one were in Scotland: moorland stretching as far as the eye can see and almost no vegetation. The salt winds here make the climate very bleak and discourage most forms of plant life; violent, whirling gusts and eddies often howl through this coastal village with its church and manor house and a few houses huddled together. Occasionally, a tree becomes bent and distorted, leaning over so far that it seems to contradict the laws of physics, the roots just managing to cling to the soil in a desperate struggle to survive. As if to make up for this, the place is blessed by an exceptional micro-climate and a mild temperature, which has allowed the original moats of the manor house to become the site of an amazing plantsman's garden.

When the originator of this garden and his wife inherited the property in 1947, there was nothing but rough grass growing right up to the moat. Over the centuries, the house had acquired a rather diverse architectural character, with the addition of other buildings, the moats and a dovecot, to the originally fortified main buildings flanking a keep. But the essential consideration in the design of the garden was the climate: on the one hand, there were the salt winds to contend with, but, on the other, mild temperatures ensured that plants which do not normally flourish in these latitudes could be grown here.

To make the most of these conditions, the garden is made up of successive enclosed spaces, screened either by the deep sides of the moat or by windbreaks based on plants, such as cordylines, eryngiums, cypress and eucalyptus, that are normally susceptible to frost in France. These provide a fairly loose structure within which the visitor wanders from space to space, discovering in each tender plants – some of which come from subtropical regions.

RIGHT
In an enclosed part of the garden, well shielded from the wind, colonies of agapanthus and silver-leaved plants surround a circular lily pond. Behind, the spiky outlines of cordylines are set against the solid round shape of a large old dovecote.

OPPOSITE
The sea provides a pale background for Echium pininana, *a plant that seeds itself prolifically. Its magnificent verticals contrast with its low-growing neighbours and the horizontal yellow line of naturalized broom, the fragrant* Spartium junceum.

No straight lines are allowed here since they do not exist in nature. The garden's charm comes from its gently curving outlines and massed effects, from loving upkeep and soft, never garish, colour schemes. A skilled botanist will discover some amazing plants, but the artistic eye is more likely to note the satisfying visual effects. One cannot fail to be fascinated by such features as the massed cortaderia, the sword-like leaves of an impenetrable phormium hedge, or a spectacular, apparently endless, green wall of gigantic gunnera. The sea can be heard but not seen until, suddenly, it comes into view, beyond a broad expanse of rough grass, on the other side of a hedge. The wind contributes its own sounds and, by parting the whippy branches of eucalyptus trees, reveals more views of the garden.

Evergreen leaves, interesting barks, shrubs and herbaceous plants grown for successive flowering mean that there is a handsome display in the garden all year round. The owners have included plants given by chance acquaintances, found when travelling, exchanged, collected, grown from seed or division. From a solitary clump of phormiums found in the courtyard a series of divisions has produced enough material for some of the enormous hedges which are now a feature of the place. Over the years the plants have been affectionately arranged and grouped into a remarkable and unconventional picture. There was never an ambitious design to follow, but the effect is extraordinarily

beautiful. The originator of the garden is no longer alive, but his wife, who played a part at every stage of its creation, and two of their children continue to add to the sumptuous plant life with the same passionate dedication.

Many of the plants that we usually cosset, keeping them in pots and taking them in for the winter, or plants we do without because they too easily succumb to cold weather, can be found here. Protected by the windbreaks, these enjoy the warmth of the nearby Gulf Stream: camellias, blue agapanthus, pink and white crinums, palms and hebes, cistus and acanthus, *Amaryllis belladonna*, warm-toned alstroemerias, bamboo and agave, dahlias

ABOVE
There can be few sights more exotic than this thicket of cordylines in flower clustering around the base of the château.

LEFT
It is hard to believe that such a rich combination of subtropical and Mediterranean plants could be displayed in such northerly latitudes, and to such harmonious effect. Here the pure white waxy flowers of Zantedeschia aethiopica *are set against the bright red jewel-like flowers of* Fuchsia magellanica, *while growing next to them are the feathery fronds of a tree fern,* Dicksonia antarctica. *The atmosphere is accentuated by the* Cordyline australis, *the cistus and the bamboo.*

left to overwinter in the soil, silver-leaved *Senecio* 'Sunshine', aloes, dimorphotheca, delicate scented geraniums. Although the cordylines here were cut down by frost in the past, they are beginning to come back from the roots and will soon be contributing again to the exotic impression the owners have taken such trouble to suggest.

Plants like these have a curious effect on the visitor, a way of transporting you to strange and unfamiliar places. There are reminiscences of Inverewe in the north of Scotland, or of Tresco off the Cornish coast. Like Osgood Mackenzie and Augustus Smith, the owners of this garden have created an extraordinary tropical landscape, their passion for plants needing warmth and light, and their stubbornness in outwitting the salt winds resulting in a luxuriant setting for a remarkable collection of plants. This is a magical place for the visitor, an astonishingly exotic demonstration of its creators' skill in orchestrating the whims of nature to their advantage.

Dreams
and Idylls

It is not too far fetched to say that these gardens offer us the chance to glimpse a more idyllic, romantic universe – they are the outcome of quests for a vision of Paradise regained. Imbued with an almost otherwordly atmosphere, each reflects the aspirations and driving forces that created it. Giverny was conceived as an Impressionist painting, conjured from pure colour, while Groussay's pavilions sprang from a longing for times past and countries far. Le Clos Normand gives us lush rose bowers, Jas Crèma scented witty inventiveness, Sardy hazy romantic images and the St Paul de Vence garden symbols of eternity. Whether their appeal is cerebral or sensual, each is suffused with a feeling of enchantment; to enter them is to enter a dream world.

Just as the pool reflects the house, so the garden at Sardy reflects the vision of its creator. Like a phoenix from the ashes, this exquisitely beautiful garden arose from a field where cattle came to drink at the duck pond. Now the pool is luxuriant with yellow flag irises, white arums and pink valerian. The cypresses make green pillars visually linking the lower garden with the house and terrace above.

Giverny

Two things were important to Monet: painting and his garden at Giverny. The two can hardly be dissociated: his pictures and garden became mutually reflecting images, twin visions that seemed to coalesce. Since he composed his garden as if it were a painting and his paintings as if planting a garden, it is impossible today to detect the boundary between the art of the gardener and that of the Impressionist painter. Monet shared his passion for gardening with his friends, particularly the writer Octave Mirbeau, and the painter Caillebotte, who had been responsible for Monet's quasi-religious conversion to gardening. 'I am glad you're bringing Caillebotte,' Mirbeau wrote shortly after Monet had bought Giverny. 'As you say, we can talk about gardening, since art and literature are so much humbug. Earth is all that matters. I've reached the point where a simple clod of earth seems miraculous and I can spend whole hours contemplating it.'

Monet had chosen to settle at Giverny because of his fascination with the landscape: the hills nearby, the orchards and poplar trees, the broad loops of the Seine and the small, scattered villages in the valley of the river Epte, all beneath the changing light from a dappled sky. The property he bought covered a little under two hectares (about four and a half acres) and included a house overlooking the road on one side and an extensive walled orchard on the other.

The layout of the garden was childishly simple, with a broad path running up the middle. Monet was scornful of the clipped box hedges and quickly got rid of them. He retained only a pair of yews and gradually replaced fruit trees with Japanese malus and cherries. He laid out a neat garden divided by regular paths, and eventually planted this with such dense masses of multi-coloured flowers that the eye ceases to notice all the angles and straight lines: the way nasturtiums are allowed to

OPPOSITE
In front of Monet's house, a dense mass of flowers overflows the traditional neat outlines of the garden. The effect is of seed broadcast in all directions: throngs of sweet rocket and honesty surround the peonies in May, while clematis scrambles up green painted supports.

RIGHT
Azaleas and rhododendrons surround the winding edge of the pool, the home of the floating water-lilies made famous by Monet's renowned series of paintings of them. Through the branches of a weeping willow, the Japanese bridge in its curtain of wisteria is just discernable.

OVERLEAF
The design of old fashioned jardins de curé (neat mixed gardens of fruit, vegetables and flowers) influenced the geometric layout of straight paths, some lined with metal arches for climbing roses. The rectilinear effect is blurred by the exuberant mixture of flowers such as irises, poppies, peonies, roses, wallflowers, honesty and sweet rocket.

spill out across the whole of the central path, for instance, positively hinders anyone trying to walk through the arches. Monet liked to grow climbing plants on these arches, gradually festooning them with roses, clematis and jasmine. Although it is abundant and luxuriant, the planting is never overwhelming as it is underpinned by the strict framework of the garden whose formality is emphasized, as in the park at Bagatelle, by standard roses planted at regular intervals. Each season produces a profusion of flowers: tulips, forget-me-nots, wallflowers, irises, poppies, sweet rocket, peonies, lupins, delphiniums, sweet peas, phlox, Japanese anemones, Michaelmas daisies, dahlias and sunflowers.

Later Monet was to acquire some land for a water garden on the other side of the Chemin du Roy, the road at the back of the property. In the pool here he planted water-lilies – yellow, white, crimson, mauve and pink – and around all the inlets and indentations along the banks informal drifts of bamboo, irises, petasites, foxgloves, azaleas and rhododendrons. And of course he built the famous Japanese bridge,

ABOVE
This path to the house runs between borders of tall bearded iris (Iris germanica) and scented yellow wallflowers.

LEFT
The immense variety of annuals, biennials and perennials creates a gloriously colourful effect. The gravel path is fringed with pink campion and the peonies have informal retinues of white and mauve rocket. The climbers on the arches will come into flower later.

RIGHT
There is a spectacular moment each year at Giverny when thousands of irises flower in an infinite range of blues, mauves, whites and browns. Here they enjoy the presence of a pale pink peony.

covering it with twining wisteria in its mauve and white forms. Monet's friend Georges Truffaut, who later became well known through his plant nurseries, was to describe the water garden in 1924, in the magazine *Jardinage*: 'The pool is fed by the river Epte and lies in a circle of weeping willows with golden-yellow branches. The land round the pool is massed with plants for acid soil: ferns, kalmias, holly and rhododendrons. Vigorous shrub roses shade the water's edge and the pool itself is planted with every known variety of water-lily.' Growing on the banks were 'the gigantic foliage of petasites, *Iris sibirica*, irises from Japan and Virginia, and *Iris ensata* (syn. *I. kaempferi*), against a backdrop of Japanese tree peonies, herbaceous peonies, groups of laburnum and Judas trees. There was also 'an extensive grove of densely planted bamboo . . . and, beside the lawns, cut-leaved thalictrum, wisteria and certain ferns with downy pink or white inflorescences. Tamarisk grows here too, and everything is interspersed with tall standard and shrub roses.' It is here that Monet was to paint the famous *Nympheas* series, and here he would constantly come

to refresh his imagination, brooding on shifting reflections in the water and the fugitive light playing through the translucent flowers and leaves.

Created between 1883 and 1926, the garden at Giverny was already famous by 1900, and Monet's gardener had five assistants under him. After the painter's death, the property was beset with family problems and over the years the garden turned into a wilderness of brambles. Gerald Van der Kemp was eventually appointed curator and in 1977 was commissioned to restore Giverny. To try and remain faithful to the spirit of the place, he often went for advice to Monet's great-nephew, Jean-Marie Toulgouat, and to André Devillers, who had known the garden in Monet's time through his visits with his boss Georges Truffaut.

The garden is resplendent once more, at its best when the long rows of bearded irises are in flower in front of the house, as Monet intended. It was from these flowers and their associations that his painting would endlessly draw inspiration. And it is his love for them which underpins the achievements of his art.

In the hills of Saint Paul de Vence

'Make me a garden to last forever'; this was the brief given by a wealthy German industrialist to landscape artist Jean Mus. It was a magnificent commission: Mus would be allowed complete freedom, with no interference in his designs; and, what is more, the client would abide by his aesthetic preferences and impose no financial limits. Here then was an extraordinary, wonderful opportunity for Mus to use all the powers of his imagination, and to bring to life ideas that – through lack of resources – had until then existed only as dreams.

When Mus was first approached in 1984 the house was surrounded by little more than a forest of pine and holm-oak; and, because it was situated close to Saint Paul de Vence, in the Provençal hills above the Mediterranean coast, the arid, sun-baked landscape and the need for a water supply – both for fertility and as a focus of pleasure – had to be taken into account.

Drawing upon an endless store of images and recollections, Mus put all his soul into the creation of the design and the garden is now a kind of entertainment, a theatrical spectacle, a walk to enchant the senses. Covering about five hectares (twelve acres), it was executed in only two and a half years. He is intensely pleased. 'The garden makes me want to shout and sing for joy, to the sound of mandolins and zithers.' The owner seems almost incredulous and his wife, too, feels, 'I can't believe all this is ours.'

A succession of changing views, sudden openings and vistas all help to catch the eye. The visitor is drawn along, enticed by scent, colour and shape, by the structured layout and the sounds of fountains and cascades. The place has an extraordinary atmosphere, like a dream landscape. Walking out of the house, the turquoise water of the swimming pool in the middle of a broad green lawn sets the tone of enchantment. A sweeping border of herbaceous plants, which curves round in thoroughly

RIGHT
Cypresses and terracotta pots overflowing with ivy-leaved geraniums border a decorative paved walk to the house.

OPPOSITE
Simple steps set like stepping stones in grass lead through a canopy of native trees to a quiet circular clearing where the darkness of the surrounding forest opens out into Mediterranean sunlight. In a scene of perfect balance between the formal and the informal, the eye is led through to the curving path on the other side by the urn on a pedestal that matches the one at the top of the steps.

English style, forms a backdrop of massed hemerocallis, azure perovskia and agapanthus. To the right, you look through to a paved pergola hung with sweet-smelling creepers, including several jasmines, for example *J. officinale affine* (syn. *J.* 'Grandiflorum') which is used for making perfumes in the nearby hills of Grasse. For conversation in the evenings, when the setting sun seems to intensify all the scents, there are inviting seats surrounded by aromatic plants. It is delightful to sit there pinching the leaves – citrus, sweet or spicy – and guess whether they are from sage, citronella, thyme or mint.

Continuing along the path, you come upon an astonishing sight: carefully graded steps that lead up to an arched arbour almost collapsing under the weight of jasmine and wisteria. The Italian effect is enhanced by vertical spires of cypress on either side. All around, carpets of pink thyme give way, in midsummer, to a sea of blue lavender, spread out under silvery olive trees. Jean Mus is particularly fond of this typically Provençal association of colours. He went to Spain, to Andalusia, personally to choose the olive trees. They all have the beautiful, charcoal-grey

LEFT
A charming stone terrace shaded from the sun and cooled by an idyllic fountain – a wall turned into a curving cascade. This watery fantasy delights the ear and eye, and pleases the flag irises (Iris pseudacorus) planted by the edge of the pool.

RIGHT
The landscape of the south has inspired this scene: carpets of wild thyme (Thymus serpyllum) in shades of mauve over the sun-baked soil. Thyme and lavender, sombre cypresses, silvery-toned olives and flowering lemon trees make a delightful, scented composition.

BELOW
This part of the garden has a wonderful sense of space. Paths lead round huge borders of ground-cover plants such as Hypericum calycinum, summer-flowering heather, lavender and Senecio 'Sunshine'. Olives, cypresses and Aleppo pines complete the picture.

gnarled and twisted trunks which great age bestows – indeed, one near the pergola is apparently more than five hundred years old – and needed enormous care to transplant.

From here you are led down through a forest of pines and holm-oaks to a circular clearing. The path in and out of this curved green 'room' is on an east-west axis so that the sun rises and sets in the clearing – a reference to the theme of eternity specified in the original commission. The dimensions of the clearing seem to be in perfect proportion to the height of the mature trees. From this point you are led on by the sound of splashing to an extraordinary scene of falling water, then on to a maze built in the woods.

The further you go from the house, the more the garden merges into the forest, with ground-cover plants which grow wild in the region. Sheets of periwinkle, rubus, fern and ivy conceal an integrated system for watering the garden and fighting the fires which can cause such devastation in the south of France.

All these delights can be enjoyed throughout the year and it is no wonder that when they are here the owners spend more than an hour every morning and evening walking round with their friends. After months spent in the grey light of inland Europe, in an industrial environment where time is of the essence, to come to this garden with its golden Mediterranean light, and its intimations of eternity, must be like stepping into quite another, enchanted world.

La Petite Rochelle

Somebody once called La Petite Rochelle a 'watercolour garden', a perfect description for a garden so astonishing in the impact of its colours that it can justifiably be called the work of an artist. House and garden are in total sympathy; blue shutters, typical of the Perche region of France, stand out above blue and pink flowers, flecked here and there with a touch of white. It is the realization of a dream, a vision that slowly materialized, shaped by time and circumstance.

From the road you would never guess what is hidden behind the surrounding walls. A little rustic gate opens to some sort of barn and, beyond this, on to the garden. Madame d'Andlau discovered the small plot of land which changed her life in 1976. She describes it as it was then: 'Behind me there was a peasant's house – long, low and grey, bare of any decorative planting, and in front of me was waste ground stretching from an old wall on one side to a sort of shed on the other, with stinging nettles and a few elderly lilacs. But at one end of this visual wilderness there were two ancient walnut trees with arching branches framing a hillside in the distance.'

In this first garden, Madame d'Andlau decided to restrict her palette to a limited colour scheme. Then, in one way and another she began to extend the garden. She concentrated next on the area just beyond the walnut trees where she made a natural-looking pool; and later she made a wild, more rustic garden beyond that. Then, using an existing walled enclosure, she made an Italian garden full of warm colours on the slope up to the house next door. Next, she determined to cultivate the area immediately in front of the house. And quite recently she started on yet another garden, called the Jardin de Solvene, as a present for her granddaughter.

The first garden, now mature, is a masterpiece. Returning to it, one can see how it has been very carefully planned in

RIGHT
The haze of pinks, blues and white perfectly complements the blue shutters and white walls of the house. The use of such a restricted palette emphasizes the different shapes and textures of an astonishing range of plants. Rock plants, including Phlox subulata, aethionema, rhodohypoxis *and blue* Linum narbonense, *and violas,* aquilegias *and* Daphne cneorum *tone with the colour of the* Ceanothus impressus *and the rose 'Neige Rose' trained up the trellis against the walls of the house.*

The predominant colour
theme of pink, blue and
white is given expression in
many different harmonious
plant associations. Here a
Ceanothus papillosus
makes a delightful
juxtaposition with a wild
soapwort (Saponaria
ocymoides) found in the
south of France.

ABOVE
In spring, the little border
in front of the house
provides a display of tulips,
the pinks and blues set off
by the rock plants and the
white exochorda blossom.

RIGHT
Wild aquilegias, which go
on seeding themselves year
after year, thrive happily in
the company of a Mollis
azalea (probably
'Berryrose') which was
given as a gift to Madame
d'Andlau.

terms of colour, structure and provision of interest throughout the year. The colours are delicate pinks and blues, making a very feminine garden. The walls of the house, once so bare, are now massed with roses ('Clair Matin', 'Charlotte Armstrong' and 'Neige Rose') and with a *Ceanothus impressus* in the same pale blue as the shutters; low plants grow at their feet and the first warm spring days bring out a mixture of tulips growing among *Phlox subulata* and the silvery foliage of lavender. Pink and white *Erigeron karvinskianus* (syn. *E. mucronatus*) spills over the steps and self-seeds every year in this sheltered spot. A low wall, built by Madame d'Andlau to break the long vista, also divides two different levels; on both sides grow her favourite daphnes and all sorts of helianthemums. Further on, a huge border runs in front of a wall, then sweeps down to a *Prunus × subhirtella* 'Autumnalis' and on towards the arching walnut trees. Opposite this lies a corresponding border, narrower in width, but in the same colours. The end is barred by a hedge, with a 'door' through which you can see the pool and its backdrop of hilly countryside.

In early summer, imagine this garden

ABOVE
The entrance to the water garden, via an archway, is defined by a pair of Tilia cordata 'Rancho' trained as standards. The area is thickly planted with shrubs and perennials that provide colour through most of the year. A second archway, enveloped in the climbing rose 'Temple Bells', leads to a wilder part of the garden.

LEFT
The sweep of the garden near the house is suffused by the whole range of pinks and blues. Sun-loving helianthemums enjoy their home in the low stone wall which divides the garden into the two levels; Rhododendron 'Blue Diamond' and tulips share a bed with other, later-flowering plants. The long undulating border on the left is balanced by another on the right and takes the eye down the slope to a pair of magnificent walnut trees and beyond them to the water garden.

with a mauve wisteria, a *Clematis montana* 'Tetrarose', the charming little deep rose flowers of *Deutzia × elegantissima* 'Rosalind', huge pale pink tree peonies, bright pink hybrid rhododendrons (the *yakushimanum* type), and pink *Cornus florida* 'Cherokee Chief', underplanted with light blue *Hyacinthoides hispanica* (syn. *Scilla campanulata*), blue irises and mauve honesty. This makes a harmonious tapestry of plants, in colours shading into each other. Other plants gradually take over: pale or deep pink lacecap and spherical hydrangeas, phlox in dots of every shade from bright pink through to violet, pale pink Japanese anemones 'September Charm', blue *Campanula lactiflora* and mauve *Thalictrum delavayi* (syn. *T. dipterocarpum*) form an equally effective picture.

All through the year there is something to be seen from the drawing room windows. In winter, the evergreen foliage of rhododendrons, pieris and daphne is a constant presence. The one inconsistency in the colour scheme comes at the beginning of spring, a time when some bright colour is desperately needed; then a brief splash of yellow – daffodils and forsythia – are allowed into the first garden.

BELOW
The garden in front of the house is flooded with white and pale yellow narcissi in spring – the only time that yellow is allowed into this part of the garden. On the right, in the foreground, is the slender vertical outline of a Prunus *'Amanogawa'.*

OPPOSITE ABOVE
The winter tracery of immaculately clipped lime trees, the starry pink blossom of a pair of Magnolia stellata *and a pair of fastigiate cherries frame the entrance to the Italian garden.*

OPPOSITE BELOW
In the Italian garden, which is formally laid out, the pale leaves of a Cornus controversa *'Variegata' – the focal point of the main vista – make a splendid contrast to the purple beech hedge which encloses the garden. Alpines, dwarf shrubs and lilies in bud give varied height in the raised beds on each side of the central path. The symmetry is emphasized by the conical evergreens, the terracotta pots and the pair of* Pittosporum tobira *'Nanum', in tubs in the foreground, which have to be brought indoors in the winter.*

Madame d'Andlau was motivated to make the Italian garden because in her first one she had no chance to use all the yellow flowers – apart from the spring bulbs – she was so fond of; now she keeps all the warm-toned colours here. Whereas a minor key had been used for the first garden's colour harmonies, a major key was chosen here: brilliant colour runs from softest, most luminous yellow in *Rosa* 'Frühlingsgold' up to the blazing bronze of *Helenium* 'Moerheim Beauty'. In between come yellow *Achillea* 'Coronation Gold', orange-toned lilies (*Lilium henryi*), and a whole range of hemerocallis, mingling with golden conifers and set against the purple prunus hedge which demarcates this garden. As with all her colour schemes, Madame d'Andlau has expanded on the central colour, using all the tones in the range from darkest to brightest, but always in small touches. She thinks that pink and yellow are raucous together; that it is dangerous to use red; and that yellow with red is unbearable. Greys and whites act as buffers, allowing all sorts of transitions and associations of colour, and are absolutely essential in avoiding clashes.

Although colour is obviously the dominant theme of La Petite Rochelle, it is a garden of different facets. Madame d'Andlau's passion for plants is important; for this, she is indebted to her uncle Prince Wolkonsky, who introduced her to some of the best plant nurseries in both France and England. She was also influenced by his poetic garden at Kerdalo, which preoccupied her for a long time. Her travels have taken her all over England, Wales, Belgium and Holland. She is never without her notebook: her garden is not static and she is always introducing new ideas.

The imagined harmonies that were the inspiration for this garden have become a reality within a firmly structured framework. The result is a superb blend of romanticism and discipline. Madame d'Andlau's life is bound up with the garden and she devotes all her attention to it, and her devotion has earned an exquisite reward. She sees the garden as a reflection of her personality and feels that it has brought her patience and perseverance, an even better knowledge of herself and greater understanding of the ways of creation. 'It is hard to follow the gardener's thoughts in this secret place or to understand his love for an ephemeral kingdom,' she explains. 'But I know that for him the garden is an image of immortality.'

Sardy

RIGHT

A luxuriant medley of roses, honeysuckle and wisteria is trained over the ochre-coloured plaster typical of houses in the Dordogne.

LEFT

The lane from the house to the meadows runs past a border thickly planted with a mixture of shrubs, perennials and biennials: roses, foxgloves, mounds of grey santolina, geraniums, pinks, philadelphus and Cerastium tomentosum. *The other side of the lane is planted in tones of blue, with* Geranium × magnificum *and nepeta set off by the white and cream spires of* Sisyrinchium striatum.

How does one define a romantic garden? A place of enchantment, with a particular haunting atmosphere apparently remote from the everyday world? Perhaps there should be a sense of fragile impermanence, as if nature is about to take over, a suggestion of mysterious melancholy, subtle light and shade, soft colours and, of course, the sound of and reflections in running water, and possibly mist to give a hazy, disembodied effect.

All these requirements are fulfilled by the Imbs's garden at Sardy, near Castillon-la-Bataille in the east of the Dordogne. Set on a sloping chalky site, the garden benefits from many natural springs but has to contend with long, dry, hot summers. The house, once the focus of a great estate, overlooks the garden from the top of a retaining stone wall, so high that it looks like a cliff face. Green pillars of Provence cypress were planted along its base to break up what would otherwise have been a dominating feature. To the right of the house the ground dips down to a channel of water, and in front it stretches out to meadows fringed with poplar trees.

The garden was made by Monsieur and Madame Imbs after they had purchased the

property in 1956. 'My father understood architecture and my mother had good colour sense,' explains Frédéric, their son who now runs Sardy, 'so they created the garden between them, with advice from Louis Aublet, an architect friend, and Jacques Desmartis, who ran a nursery garden in Bergerac.'

The Imbs knew from the outset, apparently, exactly how they would lay out the garden. They set to work at once on the big pond, where horses and cattle used to drink when Sardy was still a farm, transforming it into two long rectangles, a swimming pool in the portion nearer the house, and an ornamental pond on the far side. A bridge, now virtually obscured with two prostrate junipers, separates the two pools.

Madame Imbs had a passion for plants

ABOVE
A path, framed by arches of climbing roses and emphasized by two pairs of fastigiate cypresses which form sentinels at either end of the arcade, runs down to a fountain fed by one of Sardy's natural springs. Wild strawberries, grey Stachys byzantina *and pink valerian have colonized the steps.*

OPPOSITE
*The terrace beside the house ends in a balcony overlooking the two pools below. Pink valerian (*Centranthus ruber*) and vigorous clumps of* Corydalis lutea *have pushed their way up in front of hybrid lilies.*

and gardens. 'For her,' says Frédéric, 'gardening was a way of renewing her energy and she loved sharing this feeling with fellow enthusiasts as they walked round. The garden brought her enormous happiness.' She drew inspiration from elaborate English gardens she had known, the landscape round Florence – hence the choice of cypresses – and the gardens of Granada. The last were responsible for the formal treatment of the long channel of water which is now a home for so many plants. Beyond that, though, she worked things out instinctively, on the ground, without a paper plan. She would 'work for six hours a day on the borders, surrounded by all the plants she was so fond of, coaxing and talking to them, satisfying all their needs.' Any problems were dealt with on the spot.

BELOW
Between a pair of
Juniperus × media *is a
long vista over the pool
with its flourishing arums
and water-lilies to a hedge
with a 'bite' scalloped out of
it. In the foreground the
daisy flowers of* Erigeron
karvinskianus *(syn.* E.
mucronatus*) are growing
on the narrow bridge that
separates the swimming
pool from the ornamental
pool.*

OPPOSITE
*A yew bird perched on a
pyracantha hedge stands out
against the silvery foliage of*
Elaeagnus angustifolia. *On
the left, a venerable fig tree
makes the most of its sunny
position against a wall and
produces quantities of fruit.*
Erigeron *has carpeted the
ground at its feet.*

The structure of the garden was soon established, but the colour scheme was the result of trial and error; Madame Imbs had originally gardened near Paris and wanted to try out various improved schemes here. She particularly liked grey-leaved plants, pale colours and straightforward flowers. (Rare plants were chosen only if they could stand up to the climate.) The two sumptuous borders which line a driveway exemplify her skill and taste in planting – they are a tapestry of muted pinks, blues, mauves, silver and white in the early summer.

The property covers only half a hectare (just over an acre) but is insulated from the outside world by vines, a copse, an extensive orchard and quiet green meadows.

Standing in the lower part of the garden, one can admire the idyllic composition formed by the pool, the house and the terrace walls shrouded in luxuriant growth. Curtains of wisteria climb up the front of the house, swags of honeysuckle hang down, valerian grows in the crevices and countless daisy flowers of *Erigeron karvinskianus* (*E. mucronatus*) have seeded themselves between steps and paving

ABOVE
This path runs between the house and the rock face, and gives a view over the meadows below. Plants which enjoy the warm stone have been allowed to seed themselves between various shrubs.

PREVIOUS PAGE
Soft colours merge in the haze of a summer morning further down the lane seen on page 208. The blue in front is catmint, while pink comes from the little balls of Phuopsis stylosa *and the taller clumps of valerian. The glaucous strap leaves of* Sisyrinchium striatum *match the mound of grey santolina. This spellbinding scene is a lesson in how to weave unsophisticated plants into a web of magic.*

stones. Scent comes from the wisteria and honeysuckle, from roses and philadelphus; later, in summer, a *Clerodendrum trichotomum* growing below the house wall spreads its fragrance throughout the garden. Everywhere there is a beguiling effect of the muted colours of the flowers and grey and glaucous foliage (helichrysum, santolina, lavender, sage a *Phlomis fruticosa* and a magnificent *Elaeagnus angustifolia*).

The romantic atmosphere of the garden is enhanced by the seemingly unchecked vegetation, by the sound of running water, and, in the evening, by slanting rays from the sun which sets opposite the house. In summer, when the heat haze blurs the colours and the edges of contours, the picture is enveloped in an intangible veil.

Sardy was at its most beautiful in the early 1980s; the cold winters of 1985 and 1987 did enormous damage and killed the cypress trees. Frédéric Imbs, however, has inherited not just Sardy, but his parents' dream of how the garden should look. He is determined to restore it to its former sublimity, and he continues the work, as faithfully as possible, in the spirit of that most accomplished gardener, his mother.

Le Clos Normand

Here is a garden that achieves its sole aim – which is to be charming, simply but utterly charming. Like a miniature painting, it captivates through its richness, its clarity and its finely wrought detail.

Originally an orchard typical of those you see in Normandy near Varengeville-sur-Mer, planted with cider apple and other fruit trees under which a few cows grazed, it was turned into a garden by the owners after they decided they had had enough of watching the cows chew their way through the half dozen rose trees growing round the little barn. So the old building was turned into a weekend cottage, and in time the cob walls were boarded over. A patch of land with hawthorn bushes and what remained of the roses was fenced in to make a little garden.

Cultivating and tending this small plot soon became an obsession for Madame; gardening became so vital a part of her life that it was almost like an addiction; her mother-in-law helped by giving her another, adjacent plot of land, followed by two more; then her husband became hooked, especially on roses and clematis. As the days went by, without spending much money, the pair of them gradually created a garden of exquisite, delicate detail. Behind its decorative appearance lies a great deal of hard work, with no outside help at all. 'Sometimes we go on working in the garden till eleven o'clock in the evening,' explain the owners. 'We used only to come at the weekend, and when we came back to our plants on a Friday evening, we'd go out in the dark with torches to see how they had been getting on in our absence. Thank goodness, Varengeville gets enough rain for them not to need watering all the time.' Now they often live there during the week as well.

The style of the house made the choice of a cottage garden almost inevitable, but the owners' tastes were confirmed by many visits to English gardens, including Sissinghurst, Hidcote and Cranborne. Since the land had been acquired in stages, each new plot could become its own intimate green 'room' enclosed by hedges. Planting was to consist of a gentle mixture of roses, perennials and climbing plants; here the rose garden at Mottisfont Abbey was a decisive influence.

The house walls are devoted to delicate flowering creepers: *Solanum crispum*, both mauve and white varieties, their bell-shaped flowers appearing between soft apricot 'Gloire de Dijon' roses – 'My favourite', according to the mistress of the house, but then she is equally enthusiastic about every rose in her garden. At the base of the wall a magnificent, long-established clump of *Romneya coulteri* is clearly flourishing although carefully watched; the owners were warned to keep an eye on this plant as it can be so vigorous that suckers push through floor tiles and can take over the house. Adjoining the house is a little outdoor 'boudoir', a quiet spot surrounded by flowers. Three 'Nevada' roses stand guard, with clematis twining through their leaves (*C.* × *triternata* 'Rubromarginata').

RIGHT
A pergola surrounds the garden nearest the house and makes a romantic support for myriad flowering climbers. Rosa *'Wedding Day' cascades out of the cherry tree on the left and, from left to right along the pergola, are mounds of the charming little pale pink flowers of 'Climbing Cécile Brunner', the deeper pink of 'Mme Grégoire Staechelin', and yellow 'Elegance'. Lower down, from left to right, are shrub roses: pale pink 'Royal Highness' and orange-toned 'Charles Austin', with 'Clair Matin' just below 'Elegance'.* Lilium regale *and foxgloves grow happily between them.*

OPPOSITE
In this small garden 'room', two paths – one bordered with balls of clipped box – intersect at a stone pedestal. Shrub roses grow in colourful profusion in the borders: 'Rose Gaujard' on the left and 'Chianti' on the right. Climbing roses trail over the fruit trees ('Alberic Barbier' can be seen scrambling through an apple tree at the back), or twine over arches leading to other parts of the garden, while 'Sanders' White Rambler' makes a scented archway linking two hedges of clipped yew. Perennial and biennial flowers are encouraged to seed themselves: blue love-in-the-mist, scabious, cranebills, foxgloves and valerian are found all over the garden.

Huge pots of agapanthus (*A.* 'Isis') over-hung by a crab-apple tree, *Malus* 'John Downie', providing fruit for delicious jelly, are set on each side of a bench.

Beyond this area is the first little hedge enclosure. Inside, a pergola runs all round it, with a climbing rose and one or two clematis winding up each oak column. Mostly species clematis have been chosen as these are both easier to grow and their small flowers are more in keeping with the size of the garden. Roses such as 'Céline Forestier', 'Apple Blossom' and 'Clair Matin' mingle with *Clematis viticella*, pale pink *C.* 'Little Nell' with the tiny azure blue flowers of the *Clematis eriostemon*. At the base of the pergola, alongside a turfed walk, grow the perennials which stand out so beautifully in this context: blue nepeta, herbaceous geraniums, including the brilliant deep pink *Geranium armenum*, and the biennial foxgloves of late spring.

Inside this garden two grass paths form a cross, an old stone pedestal providing a focal point where they intersect. Regularly placed spheres of box give the design a firm framework, the sombre, static shapes contrasting with the hazy impressionistic effect of all the soft-coloured flowers. The squares formed by the cross are planted with shrub roses (both old and modern, with some English roses from David Austin), shrubs (*Buddleja* 'Lochinch', philadelphus, potentillas and *Ruta graveolens*), perennials (asters, peonies, phlox, *Viola cornuta, Campanula persicifolia* and *C. lactiflora,* white valerian), sages, artemisia, irises, pinks and bulbs, which include the ravishing *Lilium regale, Allium giganteum* and *A. aflatunense.*

Over the hedge surrounding the garden you can just see the tops of fruit trees with rambler roses scrambling through them:

LEFT
One of the many delightful old roses in the garden, the Bourbon rose 'Variegata di Bologna', has sweet scented flowers striped in pink and white.

RIGHT
A grassy path edged with shrubs and drifts of perennials entices the visitor along the pergola walk, under a canopy of intertwining clematis and roses. On the left, Clematis 'Rouge Cardinal' climbs up to meet the white climbing rose 'Herbert Stevens' at the top. Rosa 'Sombreuil' is higher still, near the middle and 'Clair Matin', covered in pale pink blooms, clambers up the further pillar. White foxgloves, hazy blue catmint and bright pink geraniums add their notes to the harmony.

OVERLEAF LEFT
The garden is reached through an orchard and a little white gate garlanded in white 'Seagull' roses. On the left of the gate is a tangle of the yellow rose 'Claire Jacquier', R. 'City of York' and the mauve clematis 'H.F. Young'. The immaculate white clematis flowers on the right belong to 'Marie Boisselot' also known as 'Mme Le Coultre'.

OVERLEAF RIGHT
This path, which crosses the one shown on page 216, runs between yet more roses: cream 'Tynwald' and wine-red 'Chianti' on the left, and 'Blairii No. 2' surging above 'Royal Highness' on the right. The path is lined with low-growing shrubs and perennials, including the arching spears of Dierama pulcherrimum foliage on the left and pale pink Crepis incana on the right. The pergola in the background is enlaced with a pale yellow climbing rose, 'Allister Stella Gray'.

LEFT

The metal frame of this archway that links two gardens is wreathed in Clematis 'Nellie Moser'. On each side are clusters of pink roses: 'Comtesse Vandal' on the left and 'Constance Spry' on the right. The path is almost blocked by blue campanula, white violas, foxgloves and pale yellow Achillea taygetea.

BELOW

A tapestry of variegated, grey and glaucous foliage encircles the base of Pyrus salicifolia 'Pendula'. The large leaves of the Hosta crispula contrast with those of the Thalictrum flavum glaucum (not yet in flower), Actaea alba, and yellow Lilium pyrenaicum, all of which are set against a backdrop of Osmunda regalis. On the extreme left are blooms of a Viburnum opulus 'Compactum'. The yew hedge provides a unifying dark background.

some of these roses are so invasive that they are beginning to stop the trees from fruiting. Nobody has yet decided which should have priority.

The great phrase here is 'there's no more room,' Monsieur explains. 'But there is always room for things you like,' Madame interrupts. This policy means that they have had to make the best of every site and use almost anything to support the roses. Sometimes roses and clematis even sprawl over the hedges. Pruning is a problem: each branch has to be untangled and laid separately on the ground, the hedge trimmed, then the roses and clematis tied back in – a feat of patience and endurance.

The next garden 'room' is reached through the most romantic gate imaginable: a gap through a yew hedge beneath a metal archway completely disappearing under the sweet-scented rose 'Sanders' White Rambler', its abundance of little double white flowers twining through a pink 'Comtesse de Bouchaud' clematis. Similar plant associations can be seen

ABOVE

Away from the house, plants are chosen for a more natural effect. A mixture of honeysuckle and a 'Léontine Gervais' rose are climbing into the central tree which has yellow day lilies at its feet. An Acer palmatum atropurpureum flourishes in the foreground, and a clipped yew hedge provides both a permanent framework and a backdrop for the generous mixed border.

around the garden: elsewhere, a Viticella clematis with small white flowers climbs through the azure blue blossom of *Ceanothus* 'Gloire de Versailles'.

As you move further from the house, you are enticed into the next green compartment by a vista leading to a very well placed, silvery *Pyrus salicifolia* 'Pendula'. Here you find a wilder type of garden and a different range of plants: hydrangeas, acers and briar roses.

With its enclosures of hawthorn and yew sheltering it from both land and sea breezes, this is an extraordinarily romantic garden. 'I often buy plants when they are in flower, and then spend a long time thinking where they'll be happiest and which plants they'll associate best with. I've acquired a lot from presents, as well as exchanges with friends,' Madame explains. It is quite obvious that this is a loved and much cherished garden, a garden of summer enchantment. A visit leaves your head full of beguiling pictures which linger long after you have gone away.

Jas Créma

At Jas Créma at the foot of Mont Ventoux in Provence, Baronne de Waldner has created a garden which conveys a strong sense of a dream brought to life. It is marked by her generous, imaginative effects, and memories of past travels, family recollections and other landmarks in a lifetime of enthusiasm are all discernible here.

The garden lies in front of a former farmhouse typical of that region, at the centre of a nine-hectare (twenty-two acre) estate planted with vines, olives, mulberry and cypress trees, with the castle of Le Barroux looming in the background. The situation is magnificent, but the climate of this part of Provence is of no help to the gardener. Summer brings pitiless sunshine and heat, with little or no rain and violent, scouring winds. In winter the temperatures drop dramatically. The extreme cold of 1985–6 killed off oleanders, rosemary and certain pittosporums, together with some roses and cordylines. But Baronne de Waldner does not let herself be discouraged: she even replants the same varieties.

When, after complicated bargaining, she finally took over the property in 1979, there was much that needed to be done. The eighteenth-century house was renovated and the mulberry avenue leading to it cut down. Baronne de Waldner sensed at once that the garden ought to be in the shape of a square and she visualized it in tones of pink, blue-mauve and white which suit the brilliant Provençal sky and blend with the traditional colours – pink and pale blue – of the house. But water and good soil were the first essentials. A water diviner eventually found a spring and, when an expropriation order closed down a farm near Le Barroux, a layer of loam was bought and carted to Jas Créma. Only at this point did the garden become a real possibility, and then the plants began to arrive. Some came from Britain because Baronne de Waldner was familiar with and

RIGHT
These old mulberry trees have been pruned into new life and now play host to climbing roses. In spring they overlook a magnificent display of shimmering irises.

OPPOSITE
When the late afternoon sun disappears behind the house, its slanting rays give a feeling of greater solidity to the contours of the garden and enhance the delicacy of the flowers. In front of the spacious Provençal house the flower garden has a colour scheme of predominantly white, grey and pink with touches of blue. Tussocks of pittosporum are growing around box that is being clipped and trained into the shape of urns, and a 'Cécile Brunner' rose is clearly flourishing on a low wall behind.

inspired by many of the finest gardens there, having lived a great part of her life in Scotland.

The visitor arrives at Jas Créma by way of a farm track running through vines and enters through the main gateway which is flanked by a pair of stone horses' heads. You are confronted first by a Banksian rose scrambling over a wrought iron frame, and then by the pink and blue house. As you walk round the left side of the building, you come upon an immense drift of blue irises, spilling down the slope – as if in some scaled-up Van Gogh painting – an intentional effect.

Along the side of the house facing the castle of Le Barroux, Madame de Waldner has built a terrace from old paving stones bought at a demolition yard. The walls are festooned in climbing roses, such as 'New Dawn', with a *Clematis montana*, a vine and *Parthenocissus quinquefolia*. Contrasting texture comes from a pair of spiky cordylines and from standard bay trees grown in terracotta pots. So lavish are the flowers of a 'Climbing Cécile Brunner' rose, that one wall seems to be on the point of collapse.

A little iron gate takes you into the first garden, where there is a formal layout of

LEFT

The terrace in front of the house has been extended to take advantage of the shade offered by two mature trees. The table and chairs, potted plants and the sound of water trickling from the dolphin-head fountain make this a delightful place to sit and look out over the garden and the village of Le Barroux.

BELOW

Baronne de Waldner is extremely fond of this charming small-flowered rose, Rosa banksiae 'Lutea' and has used it to clamber through many different shaped frames in her garden. It is thornless and almost evergreen, but not reliably hardy and has been damaged several times by the extreme weather here; but the Baronne refuses to be discouraged and replants the same variety.

straight paths running between the flowerbeds, each of which centres on a shrub pruned into the shape of an urn. Additional accents come from clipped pittosporums against a background of pinks, roses, white oleander and white agapanthus. At ground level, a framework of low arches supports the creeping miniature rose 'Nozomi'.

A second wall disappears beneath roses, this time a dense thicket of 'Mermaid'. Once past this, you are in a fragrant field of lavender, criss-crossed with paths edged in clipped rosemary. At the centre is an elephant, its trimmed box outline interwoven with the long stems of a yellow Banksian rose. This flowers in late spring, sometime after a white winter coat of *Clematis cirrhosa balearica* – which flowers for three months – has died back.

Climbing back up the hill you come to

ABOVE

The Banksian rose adorns arches in the lavender field which give it the look of a giant croquet pitch. The paths here converge on a centrepiece shaped like an elephant which, in winter, is festooned with the creamy bells of Clematis cirrhosa balearica. *'My elephant had died twice from natural causes', quips Baronne de Waldner, explaining the unreliability of the box outline. Nevertheless, she perseveres. The elephant is one of the most imaginative and personal of her ideas; she has also used it in her Paris garden.*

the swimming pool where mounds of *Pittosporum tobira* 'Nanum' are planted between the paving stones. At intervals around the edge are more stone horses' heads, also wreathed in Banksian roses. These have recently acquired plinths, bright yellow in January with *Jasminum nudiflorum*.

Back at the house, you come to an enclosed garden where box edging frames nine square beds of aromatic plants. Here Baronne de Waldner also grows an amazing collection of scented pelargoniums in pots.

Jas Créma is a garden of delight, its unaffected flowers spiced here and there with touches of Waldner imagination. Thorny weather problems are not allowed to puncture the spell. You breathe the gentlest of airs, in an enchanted, dreamlike world.

Groussay

Groussay is the expression of one man's flamboyant personality and imagination, a self-contained world built around escapism. Charles de Beistegui, its creator, was a master of illusion, a man with a penchant for drama and display; he was also a great traveller with eclectic cultural tastes. At Groussay he lived out his fantasies by constructing a series of pavilions to suggest distant times and places, linking them through landscaping so that, in effect, he turned the whole park into an open-air theatre of architectural follies.

Laid out by the Duchesse de Charost in 1815, Groussay still had an English-style park around the house when Charles de Beistegui bought the thirty-hectare (seventy-five acre) estate south-west of Paris in 1938. His own ideas gathered momentum as he gained inspiration from seeing other great gardens. Stowe in Buckinghamshire and the Désert de Retz near Saint-Germain-en-Laye had Egyptian pyramids, obelisks and a Chinese kiosk, so at Grous-

say Beistegui wanted to build a pyramid, a Turkish tent, an Italian bridge, a viewing column and a labyrinth. Helped by an architect friend, Emilio Terry, Beistegui had a plan of the estate drawn up and models constructed; Alexandre Serebriakoff made watercolour sketches. The mirage began to take shape. The pavilions themselves were built between 1958 and 1969. Every day before lunch, Beistegui would make a ritual tour of these monuments, a daily mirage of travel to distant pavilions amid herds of deer and flocks of ostriches and flamingoes.

All his pavilions alluded to the past, but Beistegui chose to interpret or decorate them in a number of fanciful ways. You come first to the blue and white striped Tartar Tent, found beyond an aviary at the end of an arcade of hornbeams. In front of it there are two parterres of box hedging interspersed with Chinese vases decorated with *trompe l'oeil* paintings. What was the source of inspiration here? Certainly Drottningholm (the Swedish Versailles) and probably also the former Pavillon de Porcelaine at Trianon because the ceiling, walls and floor inside the Tent are all tiled with modern copies of antique blue and white Delft tiles.

The Labyrinth no longer exists. But beyond the site where it stood, through a tunnel of hornbeams, you glimpse another brick and stone pavilion. Further on, statues, including those of Harlequin and Columbine, take the stage in a theatrical setting of a semi-circular green hedge. The visitor then walks down towards the river and bridge. Charles de Beistegui had lived in Venice, where he used to look down on a hump-backed bridge from his window in the Palazzo Labia, but, as he also admired Lord Pembroke's Palladian bridge at Wilton in Dorset, he made the bridge at Groussay a mixture of Palladian and Venetian styles.

When the Pyramid was built, Beistegui

ABOVE LEFT AND RIGHT
Each of the follies in the past was the product of a precise plan of campaign. The original ideas were Charles de Beistegui's. His friend Alexandre Serebriakoff would interpret these in a watercolour, which Emilio Terry would then develop as an architectural drawing. The 'Turkish Tent', made of painted metal, was based on one at Drottningholm in Sweden, a much larger building used for lodging the palace pages.

LEFT
This stone figure of Pierrot is one of the statues in the green outdoor 'theatre', a small-scale replica of one at the Villa Marlia at Lucca in Tuscany. The Italian theatre is made with yew trees, the French version a semi-circle of hornbeam.

OPPOSITE
Throughout his life at Groussay, Charles de Beistegui was motivated by the desire to create a personal Arcadia. Inspiration came from many sources – great English gardens, the Désert de Retz, the Parc Monçeau in Paris and the gardens of the Italian villas. Hornbeams are trained as straight walls or as tunnels designed to give distant glimpses of a statue or building which reveal more details as the visitor approaches. The effect works perfectly for this brick and stone temple based on those at Marlia.

OVERLEAF
The marvellous theatrical effect of this bridge over the river was achieved by moving a lifesize painting around to find the perfect site. It was designed in a mixture of styles: its low arch is based on Venetian bridges and its Palladian colonnades are like some to be found in the neo-classical garden pavilions of England.

wanted to see its reflections in a lake at all times of day. There was already one pool, but only on the east side, so he had another dug out on the west side. Against this setting the Pyramid looks magnificent, offering its mysterious inverted image in the water.

After a number of twists and turns, the path eventually leads to the Chinese Pagoda, which should really be viewed from the château. From a distance it appears to be floating on the water and unconnected to any surrounding land. To achieve this magical effect, Beistegui widened a bend in a little river which ran through the estate, then cut back a small promontory to form an island on which to set the Pagoda, linking it to the bank with a footbridge that cannot be seen from the château. The Pagoda itself is a stylized representation of China; made of wood painted to look like mahogany and maple, it appears to have eight doors but half of these are *trompe l'oeil* paintings. Set against French landscape, the very Chinese effect of the building is remarkably disorienting.

From here you go to the Column, visible from some way off and used as a viewing tower, with a staircase railed in wrought iron spiralling round the outside.

The present owner, Charles de Beistegui's nephew Juan, has recently restored the park. Most of the elms planted by the Duchesse de Charost had succumbed to disease so he has replaced them with beeches, chestnuts, plane trees and *Cupressus glabra*. In the former potager he planted a flower garden; the English designer Ian Myllis helped him achieve the colour scheme of grey, blue, green and white and the geometrical layout, following the outlines of the old kitchen garden. It is now effectively a succession of three gardens: one with borders of perennials, then a rose garden and then an ornamental potager. From here the pavilions of the park can be glimpsed above leafy branches.

Rolling lawns, winding streams, leafy enclosures and carefully placed clumps of trees provide an idyllic setting for these dream-like images of England, Italy, France, Sweden and China.

Index

Page numbers in *italic* refer to captions to the photographs.

Authors' Acknowledgments

For twenty years I have been photographing gardens, especially in France and Great Britain, both for my own pleasure and as part of my work as a photographer/journalist for the specialist garden press.

The gardens presented in this book have been selected to cover the whole range of modern French garden styles. Certain gardens no longer exist in the state in which we show them, either because the property has been sold or the owner has since died.

I would like to thank Frances Lincoln herself for having persuaded me to attempt this book on French gardens and for launching its production. I would also like to thank the whole staff at Frances Lincoln for their kindness and serious professionalism. And, of course, I would like to thank Marie-Françoise Valéry for putting into words my feelings on discovering these magical places.

Georges Lévêque

I would like to offer my most sincere thanks to the garden owners for so generously opening their gardens to me; to the designers for explaining their creative methods; to the curators and gardeners of those enchanted places; and, of course, to the whole Frances Lincoln team, with whom it has been such a pleasure to work; and last, but by no means least, to Georges Lévêque, for sharing with me the fruits of many painstaking years.

Marie-Françoise Valéry

Publishers' Acknowledgments

The publishers would like to thank the following for their help in producing this book: Anne Atkinson for translating the original French manuscript, Carole Devaney for the index, Vicky Hayward and Sarah Mitchell.
Horticultural consultant: Tony Lord
Designer: John Laing
Picture Editor: Anne Fraser
Production: Nicky Bowden
Art Director: Caroline Hillier
Editorial Director: Erica Hunningher

Gardens to visit
★ Open to specialists only
Regions are indicated in *italic type* in brackets

Apremont [*Cher*]
La Guerche- Apremont-sur-Allier
Location: 16km SW of Nevers
Opening hours: from Easter to end of September, 10–12h and 14–19h

Canon [*Calvados*]
Mézidon
Location: 20km SE of Caen
Opening hours: from Easter to 30 June; Saturdays, Sundays and holidays, 14–19h; from 1 July to 31 October; *except* Wednesdays, 14–19h and by special arrangement for groups

La Celle-les-Bordes★ [*Yvelines*]
Location; 12km E of Rambouillet

Courances [*Essonne*]
Milly-la-Forêt
Location: 18km W of Fontainebleau
Opening hours: from 1 April to 1 November, Saturdays, Sundays, 14–18h

Dampierre [*Yvelines*]
Location: 20km NE of Rambouillet
Opening hours: from 1 April to 15 October; *except* Wednesdays; 14–18h

Eyrignac [*Dordogne*]
Salignac
Location: 15km NE of Sarlat
Opening hours: from 1 July to 31 August; 14.30–18.30h; All year by special appointment

Giverny [*Eure*]
Rue Claude Monet
Location: 20km NW of Mantes-la-Jolie
Opening hours: from 1 April to 31 October; *except* Mondays; 10–18h

Les Grandes Bruyères★ [*Loiret*]
Fay-aux-Loges
Location: 25km NE of Orlèans

Kerdalo★ [*Côtes-du-Nord*]
Trédarzac
Location: 35km E of Lannion

Les Moutiers [*Seine-Maritime*]
Varengeville-sur-Mer
Location: 5km SW of Dieppe
Opening hours: from 15 April to 15 November, 10–12h and 14h to sunset

Thury-Harcourt [*Calvados*]
Location: 26km S of Caen
Opening hours: from 1 April to 30 June; Sundays and holidays, 14.30–18.30h; from 1 July to first frost, 14.30–18.30h

Le Vasterival [*Seine-Maritime*]
Sainte-Marguerite-sur-Mer
Location: 10km SW of Dieppe
Opening hours: all year for groups by appointment

Villandry [*Indre-et-Loire*]
Location: 15km W of Tours
Opening hours: all year, 9h to sunset